UNDER RECONSTRUCTION

RENEWAL AFTER RUIN

NEHEMIAH

REGULAR BAPTIST PRESS
3715 N. Ventura Drive
Arlington Heights, IL 60004-7678

The Doctrinal Basis of Our Curriculum

A more detailed statement with references is available upon request.

- The verbal, plenary inspiration of the Scriptures
- Only one true God
- The Trinity of the Godhead
- The Holy Spirit and His ministry
- The personality of Satan
- The Genesis account of creation
- Original sin and the fall of man
- The virgin birth of Christ
- Salvation through faith in the shed blood of Christ
- The bodily resurrection and priesthood of Christ
- Grace and the new birth
- Justification by faith
- Sanctification of the believer
- The security of the believer
- The church
- The ordinances of the local church: baptism by immersion and the Lord's Supper
- Biblical separation—ecclesiastical and personal
- Obedience to civil government
- The place of Israel
- The pretribulation rapture of the church
- The premillennial return of Christ
- The millennial reign of Christ
- Eternal glory in Heaven for the righteous
- Eternal torment in Hell for the wicked

Alex Bauman, editor

Under Reconstruction: Renewal after Ruin, Nehemiah
Adult Bible Study Student Book
Vol. 68 • No. 3

www.regularbaptistpress.org • 1-800-727-4440
Printed in U.S.A.

RBP0216 • ISBN: 978-1-64213-195-6

Contents

Lesson 1	Broken Leader	7
Lesson 2	Praying for Restoration	15
Lesson 3	Boldly Follow God	25
Lesson 4	Assess the Task	33
Lesson 5	Get to Work!	41
Lesson 6	Delegate!	49
Lesson 7	Facing Opposition	57
Lesson 8	Give God the Glory	67
Lesson 9	Act Wisely!	75
Lesson 10	God's Word Is Powerful	83
Lesson 11	Set the Example	93
Lesson 12	Trust and Obey	101
Lesson 13	Compromising Again	109

Preface

What does it take to become a spiritual leader? Is there a course we can take? Is there a degree we can get? Are there certain requirements we need to meet? A checklist to check off?

Nehemiah teaches us that leadership begins not with a course or a degree but with brokenness. He humbly recognized that he fell short of God's standard for His people and confessed his sin to God. That humble act opened the way for Nehemiah to become God's leader in post-exilic Jerusalem.

The book of Nehemiah records God's process of rebuilding the wall and city of Jerusalem through Nehemiah, a rebuilt spiritual leader. Nehemiah's leadership through Jerusalem's years of struggle and triumph provides an excellent example for us to follow, beginning with his brokenness.

God doesn't want us to offer ourselves to Him as a polished, self-prepared person He could use to do great things. He wants us first of all to come to Him in humility with an honest understanding of who we are and an honest dependence on Him. God is not interested in self-made leaders. He is interested in broken servants ready to be built by Him. God uses the leaders He builds as the builders in His work.

All adults are spiritual leaders to some degree. Children, young people, new believers all look to established believers for leadership. You influence people whether they realize it or not. This course is important for everyone.

Let God use the book of Nehemiah to build you into a godly leader and prepare you for the leadership roles He has for you.

Broken Leader

LESSON 1

Scripture Focus

Nehemiah 1:1–3

Theme

A spiritual leader shows concern for people and God's name.

Memory Verse

"From the end of the earth will I cry unto thee,
when my heart is overwhelmed:
lead me to the rock that is higher than I" (Psalm 61:2).

GETTING STARTED

"Don't do anything to wreck the family name!" Many a father has said that to his children. A good family name is valuable and worthy of protecting.

1. Whose family name do you highly respect? Why?

2. For whose family name do you have little or no respect? Why?

3. In what sense do you represent God's "family name"?

Nehemiah felt responsible for God's family name. He wanted it to shine for all the world to see. For that to happen, he knew God's people needed to turn to God and then rely on Him to work through them. This lesson gives us a glimpse into Nehemiah's heart for God and challenges us to share Nehemiah's concern for God's "family name."

SEARCHING THE SCRIPTURES

Repatriated Jews living in the Promised Land followed Nehemiah's leadership to reconstruct both their walls and their lives. His skills in leading God's people provide us with an example of strong Biblical leadership. This study on the book of Nehemiah will help you hone your leadership skills and will challenge you to renew your relationship with God. This first lesson presents the Nehemiah's background and the backdrop to his story.

Historical Background

Nehemiah, a Jew, served in the court of king Artaxerxes I in the Medo-Persian Empire. The Babylonian/Medo-Persian captivity had originally come upon Judah as a chastisement from God due in part to her violation of the law of the seventh-year Sabbath (Lev. 25:1–7). God warned that there would be one year of captivity for every year of failure to institute this law (2 Chron. 36:20, 21; Jer. 25:11, 12; 29:10; cf. Lev. 26:33–35). God carried out Judah's captivity in accordance with the "blessings and cursings" sections in the Mosaic Law (Lev. 26; Deut. 28) and Isaiah's prophesy to King Hezekiah (Isa. 39:7).

God used king Nebuchadnezzar of Babylon to take Judah captive. When the king first came to Jerusalem in 605 BC, it appears the Jews submitted to him without a battle (2 Chron. 36:6, 7). Thus began the first of three waves of captivity and destruction. Nebuchadnezzar returned in 597 and 586 BC to complete the captivity of Judah.

Those taken captive in 605 BC included Daniel and his three friends (Dan. 1). Those taken captive in 597 BC included Ezekiel (2 Kings 24:14–16). The final round of captivity in 586 BC affected Jeremiah who was forced to go to Egypt where he prophesied further regarding Babylon (Jer. 43; 44; 52:31–34). Babylon destroyed the city of Jerusalem and the Temple in the third wave of captivity (2 Kings 25:1–21).

Daniel 5 tells the story of the fall of Babylon to the Medes and Persians on Oct. 12, 539 BC. The Medo-Persian empire assumed control of the captive Jewish people. Truly God is in sovereign control of the nations (Jer. 18:7–10).

The Man Nehemiah

Just as there had been three waves of captivity, so there would be three waves of return. In 538 BC, Zerubbabel led the first return of roughly 50,000 Jews after the decree of Cyrus (2 Chron. 36:22, 23; Ezra 1:1–4), which had earlier been prophesied by Isaiah (Isa. 44:28—45:7).

The group that returned with Zerubbabel was significant primarily for its ultimate rebuilding of the temple in 516 BC, as prompted by the preaching of Haggai and Zechariah.

In 458 BC, Ezra led 7,000 to 8,000 Jews in the second return to the land (Ezra 7:1–10). Despite its small size, this group took part in a great spiritual revival under Ezra's leadership (Ezra 9, 10).

Nehemiah led the third wave back from captivity in 445 BC (Neh. 2). His small group was a catalyst in the enormous task of rebuilding Jerusalem's walls.

Scripture tells us nothing about the man Nehemiah outside of the book that bears his name. Surprisingly, there are no direct references to this great leader in the New Testament.

It must have been difficult for Nehemiah's parents to raise their family in a strange land. Judging by the name they gave him—"the comfort of Jehovah"—and the character traits they instilled in him, it seems evident that they were a godly couple. We know nothing of them except the testimony of their son. Effective spiritual leaders are often the product of a godly home (Ps. 127; Prov. 22:6).

4. Why would the name "the comfort of Jehovah" be a reminder of the need to show concern for others?

History can rightly be called "His story," meaning God's story. God is in control of times, events, and people. Although it seems strange that a Jew served in the court of a Persian king, it was by no means an accident.

God had Nehemiah right where He wanted him.

Nehemiah was living in the Persian king's winter palace in Shushan (Dan. 8:2; Esth. 1:2) during the month of Chislev (November/December) (Neh. 1:1). That Nehemiah was in the winter palace and close to the king indicates that Nehemiah had an important position in Persia. Just as God had put Esther on a queen's throne in Persia to deliver the Jews from wicked Haman's plot (Esther 8), so He put Nehemiah in the royal court of a Persian king to accomplish His next major step in Israel's history.

5. Knowing that God controlled key people and events in Bible history, can you safely say that He controls key people and events in your life today? Explain.

6. Why is a belief that God is sovereign such a key conviction for a spiritual leader?

7. Share an example of God's obvious working in your life.

The Setting

Nehemiah's inquiry into the state of the people in Jerusalem (Neh. 1:2) came ninety-two years after Zerubbabel first led a return of captives back to Jerusalem. During those years, God used Persian kings to accomplish His plan to repopulate and restore Judah. God's pattern continued in Nehemiah's day. He planned to use Artaxerxes I to further His plans to strengthen Judah.

Hanani, Nehemiah's brother, and others from Judah visited Nehemiah in the king's palace. Some commentators believe that Hanani, meaning "the grace of the Lord," came from Jerusalem on business unrelated to Jerusalem's condition. The text explains neither the timing nor the nature of his trip, so we don't know for sure why he went to Jerusalem or why he came back to see Nehemiah.

Nehemiah asked about Jerusalem and its residents (1:2). His questions reveal his genuine interest in and concern for God's people. His concern was driven by his desire to see God's people glorify God's name once again. Nehemiah could have been proudly content with his noble position in Persia and disinterested in Jerusalem and the needs of those less fortunate. This was not in his character, however. God's glory was at the forefront of his mind.

8. Put yourself in Nehemiah's place. What thoughts and feelings would you have in your comfortable situation upon learning about the plight of your fellow Jews in Jerusalem?

9. What might happen to the ministry of a spiritual leader who does not have the qualities of genuine interest and concern for others?

Challenge 1: Affliction

Hanani did not merely say the Jews back home were afflicted, he reported that they were "in great affliction" (1:3). Hanani used a term with the root idea of "evil." In other passages the term conveys physical pain (Num. 16:15; Ps. 105:15). Sometimes it bears the idea of emotional pain (Gen 43:6; 1 Kings 17:20). In Ruth 1:21, the word describes the physical and emotional pain Naomi experienced in losing her family.

Nehemiah's kindred in Judah wrestled against discouragement and danger. Their enemies hassled them relentlessly, using political and military pressure to crush their rebuilding efforts. In addition, their disobedience to God caused them discomfort too.

Challenge 2: Reproach

The Jews in their homeland were also in "reproach" (Neh. 1:3). To be in reproach means to be disgraced. The Jews boasted of their glorious and faithful God, but their land still lay in ruin. Their apathy and neglect gave God a bad name. It appeared to the Jews' enemies that God was a rather pathetic, anemic God. If their God was so great, why didn't they rebuild their city? Why was God's temple still surrounded by ruins left from an invasion that happened decades earlier? Hanani understandably felt embarrassed by the lack of progress in Judah. We know from the prophet Haggai that the repatriated Jews wouldn't have even built the temple if it weren't for Haggai's preaching (Hag. 1:2–5).

10. Read Haggai 1:3–15. Summarize Haggai's message to the remnant of Jews living in the land.

11. What was the result of his message?

12. Why is a desire to glorify God such a necessary quality in a spiritual leader?

Challenge 3: Disrepair

Hanani's report included a reference to Jerusalem being "broken down" (Neh. 1:3). Was Hanani's report just a rehearsal of what happened to Jerusalem in 586 BC when the walls and gates were breached and the temple burned by the Babylonians? Most likely not, for Nehemiah had a strong response to Hanani's report, suggesting he hadn't heard the news before (1:4).

From the book of Ezra, we can conclude that Hanani's report referenced a more recent breaking down of Jerusalem's walls. Ezra wrote a list of oppositions to the rebuilding progress in Jerusalem (Ezra 4:6–23). The opposition under Artaxerxes I king of Persia is most likely the news that discouraged Nehemiah (4:7–23). Artaxerxes I reigned from 465-425 BC.

During Artaxerxes' reign, the repatriated Jews in Jerusalem went further than the edict of Cyrus (538 BC) had allowed and began rebuilding the city walls instead of just the temple. When their enemies, Samaritans named Rehum and Shimshai, came to realize this, they alerted king Artaxerxes I. They wrote a letter to the king warning him that a rebuilt Jerusalem would doubtless be a threat to his power (Ezra 4:12–16). Artaxerxes sent a letter in reply, forcing the Jews to stop rebuilding until he issued any additional directions (4:21). Emboldened, the Samaritans went beyond the intentions of the king's letter and mounted an attack upon the Jews, destroying the newly rebuilt sections of the Jerusalem wall (4:23). The loss likely drained the Jewish settlers of all hope and robbed them of a significant portion of their resources.

The news of this more recent devastation in Jerusalem moved Nehemiah to tears and prayer for his people. He certainly encountered "troublous times" as Daniel predicted (Dan 9:25). God's temple and people were left seemingly defenseless.

13. Of what did the broken walls remind the Jews?

14. In what way were the broken walls a symbol of what needed to happen to Jerusalem's leaders and people? What "walls" in their lives needed to be broken down for the rebuilding of the physical walls to begin?

Nehemiah could have easily ignored his homeland. Afterall, he enjoyed the comforts of palace life in Persia. His love for God and God's people, however, prevented him adopting such an insensitive response. His heart ached for God's people and God's name. In the coming accounts, we will learn that he risked his life to restore both to their former glory. Of course, God proved faithful once again as He responded to Nehemiah's deep faith.

MAKING IT PERSONAL

15. Name some people who look to you as a spiritual leader.

16. What do your efforts as a spiritual leader say about the level of concern you have for those following you?

17. How do your efforts as a spiritual leader reflect on God's name? Do your actions glorify God? In what ways?

18. What are some ways you could increase your concern for those you are responsible for leading?

19. What are some ways you could increase your concern for God's name and reputation?

Praying for Restoration

LESSON 2

Scripture Focus

Nehemiah 1:4–11

Theme

God wants us to own our sin, confess it, and take restorative steps.

Memory Verse

"And it came to pass, when I heard these words, that I sat down and wept, and mourned certain days, and fasted, and prayed before the God of heaven" (Nehemiah 1:4).

GETTING STARTED

Children sometimes have an inflated sense of their ability to hide their guilt, even when the evidence of their guilt is literally all over their faces.

1. When have you caught a child "red-handed"?

2. How did the child respond?

God caught Nehemiah and the repatriated Jews in Jerusalem red-handed. Instead of denying their sin problem, Nehemiah owned it, asked God for forgiveness, and then offered himself to God to use in the restoration process. His response to sin should encourage us to take similar steps.

SEARCHING THE SCRIPTURES

Upon hearing bad news from Jerusalem, Nehemiah was brokenhearted. One can clearly see his love for God's reputation and for God's people. His weeping displayed strong emotion (Neh. 1:4). His mourning demonstrated compassion and empathy. His fasting required personal sacrifice. His praying, however, revealed his heart of trust and confidence in God.

Nehemiah Recognized Sin's Offensiveness

As Nehemiah considered the incredible significance of Hanani's report about the conditions in Jerusalem, whereby newly rebuilt walls had recently been torn down and newly hung gates had been burned, he channeled his concern into prayer to the Lord.

Nehemiah demonstrated spiritual sensitivity as he prayed to the sovereign God (1:4). He paused in broken dependence upon the Lord. His sensitive prayer shows us the incredible importance of having a burden for the work of the Lord if we are to succeed in making an impact for God in the world.

3. Read Nehemiah 1:4. How would you describe Nehemiah's attitude as he began to pray to God?

Nehemiah sat down and wept because he understood the bad report from Jerusalem signified a sin problem among God's people. God allowed the newly rebuilt walls to be torn down and the gates to be burned because His people needed to seek His forgiveness and ask Him for personal restoration.

God's covenant relationship with Israel tied their prosperity and safety in the Promised Land to their obedience to Him (Deut. 28). The wall failed because the people failed to obey God. The broken wall and burned gates were physical representations of Israel's broken relationship with God.

God spelled out His treatment of His people in the Old Testament law of retribution, a part of the Mosaic Covenant. God promised to bless His people and land if they lived righteously (28:1, 2). If they disobeyed, they would experience God's chastisement (28:58, 63).

In this age, we don't have a Mosaic Covenant with God tied to our quality of life in a particular piece of land. In fact, we might be living obediently to God and suffer physical or financial problems as a result (1 Pet. 3:13–15). Peter counted such suffering a privilege and a reason to rejoice. That type of suffering is not what the Jews were experiencing. They suffered because they sinned.

The seriousness and offensiveness of sin transcends all times. When we know we have sinned, we ought to sit and weep like Nehemiah did. Sin always offends God and destroys our personal relationship with Him, putting a halt to our spiritual growth and effectiveness as servants of God.

4. For what do you think Nehemiah mourned, or showed regret?

Sin always robs us of what could have been. No doubt Nehemiah considered the poor testimony of Jerusalem's broken walls and burned gates. The city should have been a beacon to God's greatness. Instead, God's name suffered greatly while His disobedient people cowered behind their ruins. Israel's enemies laughed at the repatriated Jews and boldly challenged God while seeming to get away with it.

5. What precautions should believers take when weeping over sin and mourning the hurt and loss it caused?

While Nehemiah mourned for a season, he didn't spiral into depression and hopelessness. Refusing to be paralyzed by deep regret, he turned to God, his only hope.

Nehemiah Acknowledged God's Greatness

While the Jews' obedience to God ebbed and flowed, God's greatness remained the same. He doesn't have lapses or bad days. He neither makes wrong decisions nor forgets to do right. Nehemiah recognized God's faithfulness to His holy, loving character as he opened his prayer to God for restoration.

6. Read Nehemiah 1:5. What aspects of God's greatness are important for the repentant sinner to remember?

Nehemiah stated that God keeps His covenant with His people. The word he used for "keep" has as its root a word that means "guard" or "keep safe." Later in verse 5, Nehemiah said that God gives mercy and love to those who love God and "observe" God's commandments. The word for "observe" comes from the same root as the word for "keep." Nehemiah recognized that God stayed faithful to His promises even though His people abandoned Him. Nehemiah also recognized that God's offer of mercy still stood. If God's people turned to Him for restoration, God would pour out His mercy into their lives and forgive their sins.

7. What word comes to mind when you think of God's mercy?

Nehemiah Requested God's Forgiveness

As Nehemiah began to formulate his request to God, he displayed repentance over "the sins of the children of Israel" (Neh. 1:6). He included himself as a sinner in need of forgiveness. He was not self-righteous or haughty.

The Hebrew word for "confess" means "to hold out the hand or to reveal" (1:6). The opposite idea would be to keep to oneself. Nehemiah essentially held out his sin-stained hands for God to see and cleanse. Of course, trying to hide one's sin from God is ridiculous, for He sees and knows all. Denying our sin is as silly as a child denying he was digging in his mom's flower garden when his hands and shirt are covered in dirt.

8. Why might a person be tempted to think he could hide his sin?

Nehemiah understood that God had been terribly offended. He committed himself to praying "day and night" for the restoration of himself and God's people (1:7). He confessed that he and the people had "not kept the commandments, nor the statutes, nor the judgments" that God gave to Moses. These terms are not simply synonyms. The law Moses received from God can be understood in three parts: the moral law (e.g., the Ten Commandments), the civil law (domestic regulations), and the ceremonial law (instructions pertaining to the sacrificial system, tabernacle/temple, and priesthood). Nehemiah confessed that Israel had violated all three of these aspects of the law. By confessing his own sins and the sins of Israel on their behalf, Nehemiah was fulfilling the requirement to "return unto the Lord" (Deut. 30:2).

9. Read Deuteronomy 30:1–3. What requirement shows that God demanded sincere repentance?

Like Daniel (Dan. 9), Nehemiah prayed for the nation according to passages such as 2 Chronicles 7:14, confessing national sins and asking for revival. There is no practice in the New Testament which corresponds to this type of repentant prayer. We may nevertheless learn from Nehemiah's experience and allow his example of fervor, sincerity, and intercession to shape our personal prayer and devotional lives. God still requires us to approach Him with sincerity when asking for His forgiveness of our sins.

Nehemiah Appealed to God's Faithfulness

Nehemiah knew the Law of Moses thoroughly. He knew the passages that taught the retribution principle (Deut. 28:63–67), and he also knew the promises of restoration taught in the same Mosaic Covenant (30:1–5). This covenant relationship with God provided the basis for his petition. He asked God to honor the promises He made through Moses to restore and bless His people as they returned to Him.

As Nehemiah rehearsed God's promises, he pleaded with God to remember the word that He had given His servant Moses (Neh. 1:8). Certainly, God does not forget. Nehemiah meant that he was taking God at His word. He was basing his appeal on God's promise to restore His people to the Promised Land if they turned from their sins with all their hearts.

Notice in Nehemiah 1:9 that Nehemiah included that God put Israel in the Promised Land as a dwelling for God's "name." God would always be faithful to His people because His reputation was on the line. God's faithfulness, though, goes both ways. He faithfully drove His people from their land when they disobeyed and faithfully began to bring them back when they turned to Him. God's name was glorified in both cases.

God's faithfulness should cause us to both respect Him and rejoice in Him. He will be faithful to chasten us when we wander from Him and faithful to restore us when we turn to Him (Heb. 12:3–11).

10. When have you been glad God faithfully drew you back to Himself?

Nehemiah Reminded God of Past Redemption

Nehemiah, having prayed about personal restoration, turned his attention to the physical restoration of Jerusalem. Jerusalem's broken walls and burned gates needed attention.

Nehemiah recalled God's redemption of Israel in the past (1:10; cf. Deut. 9:29). Israel wasn't a desirable people from the world's perspective. They were a nobody nation living as slaves in Egypt. God chose to redeem Israel because He loved them and wanted to show the world His redemptive power. Nehemiah wanted God to continue to act according to that same redemptive love. Of course, Nehemiah had no doubt that God could restore Israel and provide for the physical rebuilding of their walls and gates.

11. How does remembering the price of your redemption affect your hope in God?

Nehemiah Requested God's Present Intercession

Accentuating the earnestness of his request, Nehemiah offered himself before the Lord to be a part of the answer. He requested that God would "prosper" him (Neh. 1:11). By using the words "your servant," Nehemiah placed himself in the hands of God to be used as God saw fit. From merely a human perspective, he was taking a risk by turning himself over to God. His life at Susa was comfortable. His routine was established. He had vocational security for a lifetime. Yet he saw that his spiritual homeland languished, and he willingly sought a way to help the situation. His prayer for prosperity was not a selfish request for personal success. He sought for success in accomplishing the will of God.

The remainder of the book of Nehemiah is the story of what people can accomplish in the work of God when they give themselves completely over to the Lord for His service.

12. When have you responded to a need by offering yourself to God to accomplish His will in meeting the need?

Nehemiah asked God to prosper him "this day." It is easy to put off urgent matters that require great personal sacrifice. Nehemiah was willing to be used at once. This, again, demonstrates the genuineness of his prayer. No wonder Nehemiah became a great spiritual leader.

Nehemiah further asked God for "mercy in the sight of this man," meaning king Artaxerxes I, for he "was the king's cupbearer." As the king's personal cupbearer, Nehemiah was with the king of the Medo Persian Empire continuously. The cupbearer shielded the king from being poisoned. He tasted the king's food and drink before the king partook of it. We may infer from the context of the next chapter that, in the course of performing his duties, Nehemiah had become a trusted and valuable advisor to the king. Nehemiah would not have been in this position if he were not a man of unquestioned loyalty and integrity.

The mighty King Artaxerxes I had the authority to decree the reconstruction of Jerusalem. But it was against Persian protocol for the cupbearer to make a request before the king. The seriousness of this matter was intensified because earlier this same king had issued a decree ordering a suspension of Jerusalem's reconstruction (Ezra 4:21).

13. Nehemiah was obviously fearful of the prospect of making a request of the king. What responses could Nehemiah have had instead of praying about the difficult task?

14. What is your typical response when you are faced with a difficult task as you serve God?

It is significant that God sovereignly placed Nehemiah under the only man in the Persian Empire who could reverse his own decree! Nehemiah knew that God moves the hearts of kings (cf. Prov. 21:1). So, he prayed for mercy in this king's eyes. Here again is this wonderful balance of divine sovereignty and human responsibility.

We may wonder for how long Nehemiah prayed. According to verse 4, it was for "certain days." Verse 6 says that he prayed "day and night" during this time. But when we turn to chapter 2, we learn that his season of prayer lasted roughly four months, until the month of Nisan, or March/April, of 445 BC. What an intense, single-minded burden he had for the work of the Lord!

MAKING IT PERSONAL

15. How have you responded to adversities? Has prayer been one of your responses?

16. Why is prayer the right response to the adversities you face?

17. Do you have any unconfessed sin in your heart that might be responsible for your adversity? If so, confess it, and invite God's cleansing and forgiveness (1 John 1:9).

18. What promises of God do you need to stand on as you take your requests to Him?

Boldly Follow God

Scripture Focus

Nehemiah 2:1–8

Theme

God wants us to trust His power and sovereignty as we boldly serve Him.

Memory Verse

"So that we may boldly say, The Lord is my helper, and I will not fear what man shall do unto me" (Hebrews 13:6).

GETTING STARTED

One little kid included giant cockroaches on his Christmas wish list while another asked for a yak and "100 yak food." They obviously weren't shy about asking for these they had no chance of getting.

1. What is the biggest gift you asked your parents for when you were growing up?

2. How bold were you in your asking?

3. What did your parents think about your request, and did they grant it?

Nehemiah made a request of a king that could be described as asking for the moon. Such a request took the boldness that God granted him.

God expects us to be bold in our service for Him. Fears or inhibitions are not valid excuses for failing to serve Him boldly.

SEARCHING THE SCRIPTURES

After praying for God's forgiveness and blessing toward the people of Israel, Nehemiah asked God for an opportunity to speak to the king about Jerusalem's plight. Nehemiah 2:1–8 explains how God answered Nehemiah's prayer.

God's Perfect Time

In the month Chislev (November/December) Nehemiah asked God to prosper him "this day" (Neh. 1:1, 11). God answered Nehemiah's request, however, in the month Nisan (March/April; 2:1), four months later (2:1). Think of the dedication Nehemiah showed in praying for his people for four months. Often, man's timetable doesn't match that of the all-wise God. God answered Nehemiah's prayer in His good time, and Nehemiah remained faithful until then.

4. Read Psalm 37:5. Relate incidents in which God answered your prayer according to His timetable rather than your own.

God may have begun answering Nehemiah's prayer on the day Nehemiah uttered it by cultivating a special rapport between the king and Nehemiah. By the time the events of chapter 2 occurred, the king was evidencing significant respect for and sensitivity toward Nehemiah.

Nehemiah's Fear

God answered Nehemiah's prayer in an unusual way. One day, when Nehemiah presented a cup to the king, the king observed that Nehemiah looked sad (2:2). His "countenance" clearly displayed the results of four months of anguished, persistent prayer.

Ancient kings were not accustomed to anyone being sad in their sight and did not tolerate it, as it could be a sign of bad news or palace intrigue. Furthermore, the king had enough of his own problems without caring for those of his servants.

Nehemiah had not previously been distressed in front of the king (2:1). When the king asked Nehemiah why he looked sad, Nehemiah became deeply afraid. He knew that such behavior was contrary to Persian law and protocol and that the king held the power of life and death over him.

5. Is it all right to feel fear even while trusting God? Explain.

6. Share experiences from your own life when you were trusting God while still experiencing the human element of fear.

Nehemiah's sad appearance seems intentional. It appears he let his sadness show so he might have an opportunity to speak to the king about the plight of Jerusalem. If he didn't somehow spark the conversation about Jerusalem, then the topic probably would have never come up.

Nehemiah wanted the conversation to start so he could ask the king to order the rebuilding of Jerusalem, a reversal of the king's earlier decree. The king had previously ordered all work on the Jerusalem wall to cease (Ezra 4:21).

Nehemiah's Wisdom and Boldness

Nehemiah could have cowered and denied at the last minute that he was sad, but he viewed the king's question as God's open door instead. He took his life in his hands and went through the open door, answering the king wisely and boldly. He courageously told the king that the place of his forefathers' graves was in ruins (2:3).

Nehemiah's response reveals his discretion and sensitivity to the Persians' practice of honoring their dead ancestors and carefully preserving their graves. He mentioned his ancestors to gain king Artaxerxes's sympathy. Furthermore, Nehemiah avoided directly referencing Jerusalem to avoid political connotations. As such, Nehemiah exercised remarkable prudence, a sign he had probably researched Artaxerxes's previous statement on the matter of rebuilding Jerusalem (Ezra 4:21).

7. Read Ezra 4:17–22. What reasons did the king originally give for not allowing the rebuilding of Jerusalem's wall?

8. How does the list of reasons help you appreciate the boldness Nehemiah had when he made his request before the king?

9. How does the list of reasons help you understand the boldness God could require from you?

God's Control

King Artaxerxes did not punish Nehemiah for his open expression of sorrow. Instead he asked Nehemiah how he could help him (2:4). The king's unexpected response is a testimony to God's control over the king.

10. Read Nehemiah 2:4. How did Nehemiah demonstrate his dependence on God?

11. How does Nehemiah's immediate response to the king's question help you understand boldness? Is boldness a brave performance a person puts on, or is it a humble submission to God to follow His leading no matter the circumstances?

Remember that Nehemiah's short prayer before answering the king built on four months' worth of Scriptural, heartfelt, intense prayer. He had prepared himself for this moment by putting his trust in God into practice.

Nehemiah's Request

Nehemiah began his request with the utmost respect and courtesy. "If it please the king," he offered. He then kept his request brief and to the point, respecting the king's time. The king responded tersely as did most decision makers of his day.

Nehemiah also showed respect by referring to himself as the king's servant. By doing so he acknowledged his subservient role in the kingdom and the king's authority and power. A proud man might have touted his own official position, political connections, or service record.

12. Read Matthew 23:12. What principle does this verse teach?

13. From what you already know about the book of Nehemiah, how do you see this principle demonstrated in Nehemiah's life, particularly in his relationship with God?

We should recognize that Nehemiah was willing to leave his important role as a trusted advisor to the king to go and rebuild the broken-down city of Jerusalem (Neh. 2:5). His request could be compared to a president's cabinet member requesting to leave the White House to lead a difficult renovation project using a band of misfits in a dangerous, enemy-infested land. Yet, that's what Nehemiah was willing to do. His said, "that *I* may rebuild it."

Perhaps the king was touched by Nehemiah's willingness to take on such a difficult task. No doubt he respected Nehemiah's willingness to sacrifice himself and give up his privileges to help his native people. And if Nehemiah was so selfless, then the repatriated Jews must not be the scoundrels the Samaritans had made them out to be (Ezra 4:11–16).

Nehemiah's request also brought to light that the Samaritans who received the cease and desist order from the king had overstepped the king's authority in the order by burning the Jews' newly hung gates and breaking down their newly repaired walls (Ezra 4:23). With his own personal testimony providing credibility for the Jews, Nehemiah in essence presented the case that Judah's enemies were also the king's enemies and that the Jews were truly the king's loyal servants and allies.

Nehemiah must have also picked up on the fact that the king ordered the Jews to stop building the city and walls "until" he gave them the order to do so. "Give ye now commandment to cause these men to cease, and that this city be not builded, until another commandment shall be given from me" (Ezra 4:21). Nehemiah jogged the king's memory and hoped God might prompt the king to give that order sooner rather than later.

The King Authorized Nehemiah's Plan

The note that the queen was present when the king gave his answer is unusual and likely significant (Neh. 2:6). Perhaps the writer implied that Artaxerxes's queen was sympathetic to the Jews because of the effect that her mother-in-law, Esther, had upon her. We are left to wonder if the queen had come to respect, or even to personally believe in, the God of Israel. Whatever the case, the seemingly impossible occurred, and Nehemiah seemed to draw a connection between the queen's presence and the king's decision.

After asking Nehemiah how long the journey to Judah would take and when he would return, the king granted him permission to go (2:6). The fact that Nehemiah was quick to give the king his proposed timetable is yet another indication of his thoughtful planning during the intervening four months.

14. How do you think Nehemiah felt as the king gave him permission to return to Judah?

Nehemiah's trip back was more than seven hundred miles and would take at least four mouths roundtrip, but he certainly never envisioned that he would be gone for twelve years (5:14; 445 to 433 BC). If he did, then the king's permission is even more amazing.

Nehemiah demonstrated further boldness and forethought as he made an additional request of the king. Knowing that the Jews had many enemies throughout the regions west of the Euphrates River, he asked for documents of authorization that he could present to the governors of each region (2:7). Such documents would guarantee him safe passage through those tenuous lands.

Sensing the full support of the king, Nehemiah asked for timber from the king's forest that could be used in the construction effort. Again, we see evidence that Nehemiah had put a plan in place in case the king gave him a positive response.

God Orchestrated His Greater Plan

15. Read Nehemiah 2:8. Why was Nehemiah so bold in asking the king "for the moon"?

King Artaxerxes granted Nehemiah the additional requests for safe passage and the king's timber. Nehemiah explained why in verse 8. It was "according to the good hand of my God upon me." Although Nehemiah used great patience, wisdom, and boldness, he knew God had graciously blessed him.

As the king spoke this word, God's prophetic clock began to tick. Nehemiah's burden fit providentially into God's prophetic plan for Israel as revealed to the prophet Daniel.

Daniel 9:24–27 gives the timetable for God's dealings with Israel. These verses tell precisely when the Messiah would come and suffer crucifixion. The verses also speak of the destruction of Jerusalem, which has happened, and the still future Great Tribulation.

Daniel 9 is part of Gabriel's revelation to Daniel. The period Gabriel spoke of is seventy weeks, or "seventy sevens." There are seventy "weeks" that are each seven years long. The total time referred to in Daniel's prophecy then is 490 years.

What started the clock ticking on these 490 years? It was "the going forth of the commandment to restore and to build Jerusalem" (Dan. 9:25). So far, 69 of the 70 weeks have passed. The final "week" is the seven-year Great Tribulation that begins shortly after Christ raptures the church (1 Thess. 4:16, 17). Only God the Father knows when He will send Christ for His church and begin that final week in Daniel's prophecy (Mark 13:32–37).

Nehemiah grew bold because he trusted God to work His plan without fail. He witnessed the beginning of God's grand timetable that will usher in the end times. We are now waiting for that timetable to restart. In the meantime, we ought to be serving God with boldness, knowing that God is still on His throne and that He could send His Son at any moment to get us and take us to Heaven.

MAKING IT PERSONAL

16. What requests, if any, are you waiting for God to answer?

Although God sometimes answers with an immediate yes or no, He sometimes wants us to wait for His perfect timing. Put your requests into His hands and wait patiently for Him.

17. What fearful challenges might you face?

18. There are no excuses for not following God's lead in our lives. What are some excuses we might use anyway?

19. Ask God for holy boldness and the ability to exercise it wisely for His glory.

Assess the Task

Scripture Focus

Nehemiah 2:9–16

Theme

A spiritual leader assesses the needs before he begins a task.

Memory Verse

"The thoughts of the diligent tend only to plenteousness; but of every one that is hasty only to want" (Proverbs 21:5).

GETTING STARTED

Nelaton was a skilled and widely esteemed French surgeon. Once he said that if he had only four minutes to perform a life-saving operation, he would take at least one minute to assess the best way to do it!

1. How would you feel if your surgeon said he was going to plan your surgery "on the fly"?

2. What other jobs demand careful assessment of circumstances in order for the worker to be successful?

Nehemiah took time to carefully assess the circumstances he was in. He understood the problems well enough to begin to plan for solutions.

SEARCHING THE SCRIPTURES

When facing a project, a leader needs to understand what ought to be done, what can be done, and how to do it. Having heard the report of his brother, Hanani (cf. Neh. 1:1–3), Nehemiah knew what had to be done. The walls and gates of Jerusalem needed to be rebuilt. So, Nehemiah needed to find out what he could do and how he could do it. Obviously, He had to go to Jerusalem for himself; he could not manage a task of such magnitude from a distance. He needed to see the situation firsthand so could do a proper assessment.

Following four months of intense prayer, the king had granted Nehemiah's request to return to Jerusalem and undertake this great work in fulfillment of Daniel 9:25. Gabriel had revealed to Daniel that the seventy prophetic weeks (490 years) in Israel's prophetic future would begin at the time "of the commandment to restore and to build Jerusalem."

All the difficult rebuilding tasks lay ahead of Nehemiah. Dealing with the powerful, well-organized enemies in and around Judah lay ahead of him too. God provided the resources for building. Nehemiah knew God would take care any enemy resistance too. God's hand was on Nehemiah (2:8).

Letters to the Governors

The trip from Persia to Jerusalem was an amazing undertaking in Nehemiah's day. He had to pass through numerous provinces in the Trans-Euphrates region before he ever reached Judah. Even if Nehemiah took the shortest route from Susa to Jerusalem, it would have taken at least two months to make the roughly 800-mile journey. This route ran through Babylon, up the Euphrates River, over to Damascus, southwest through Samaria, and then due south into Jerusalem.

Nehemiah requested letters of authorization from King Artaxerxes I to show to the governors in the Trans-Euphrates region (2:7, 9). The king willingly granted the letters. Nehemiah showed these documents to all the governors along the way. This resulted in his safe passage.

3. Was Nehemiah showing a lack of trust in God by asking the king for the letters of safe passage? Explain.

Protection from the King

While 50,000 Jews returned with Zerubbabel in the first return from Persia to Jerusalem (538 BC) and several thousand more Jews returned with Ezra in the second return (458 BC), Nehemiah was possibly the only Jew who went to Jerusalem in the third return (445 BC). He did not make this journey alone. He reported, "Now the king had sent captains of the army and horsemen with me" (2:9).

As the king's cupbearer, Nehemiah customarily received military protection whenever he traveled on official royal business. Nehemiah's trip to Jerusalem, however, was not an official royal trip. That the king gave him a military escort anyway is another testimony to God's goodness, for the king didn't like Jerusalem and wouldn't have been inclined to provide anything extra to ensure its revival.

Ezra, who returned under very different circumstances at a different time, took a different approach when dealing with the same king (Ezra 8:22, 23).

4. Read Ezra 8:22, 23. Nehemiah's use of human protection and Ezra's rejection of human protection stand in contrast. Was Ezra's faith stronger than Nehemiah's? Explain.

Both Ezra and Nehemiah were men of faith. What the one rejected because of faith the other accepted as from the Lord. If Nehemiah had rejected all military assistance, he would have travelled alone. Ezra, by contrast, had thousands of traveling companions. Furthermore, Nehemiah needed help to transport the materials and travel rations.

Nehemiah's Potential Adversaries

God's work never goes unopposed, and Nehemiah witnessed that as he neared Jerusalem. Sanballat and Tobiah were poised to be major threats to Nehemiah's building project (2:10). Nehemiah sensed their animosity toward him as he traveled through their region.

Sanballat was a Horonite, probably from Haran in Mesopotamia. Haran was the center of moon god ("Sin") worship. "Sanballat" was a

Babylonian name meaning "the god Sin has given life." Sanballat is identified in history as the governor of Samaria.

Tobiah was an Ammonite and therefore a descendant of Lot's younger daughter. "Tobiah" is a Hebrew name that means "Yahweh is good." Ammon was a region southeast of Samaria, beyond the Jordan River. Ammonites worshiped the false god Moleck. Tobiah was a servant of the King of Persia and was identified in history as the governor of Ammon.

Sanballat and Tobiah are illustrations that Satan always exerts his influence to oppose the work of God. Satan used Sanballat and Tobiah because they were open to his insidious methods. When they heard of Nehemiah's purpose, "It grieved them exceedingly that there was come a man to seek the welfare of the children of Israel" (2:10). They hated the Jews and were happy to see the Jews' capital city in ruins. To them the ruins testified that God is weak and disinterested in His people. Nehemiah's presence and train of timber and soldiers revealed that Tobiah and Sanballat's understanding of God might be wrong. The possibility that God might yet love His people and work to revive their city caused them great grief.

5. Why would Sanballat and Tobiah be so opposed to Nehemiah and the rebuilding of Jerusalem?

6. What might Nehemiah have wrongly concluded based on the presence of strong opposition in the area?

Nehemiah's Patient Assessment

Nehemiah had first heard about Jerusalem's plight in November or December and received opportunity in March or April to make his request to the king. If he left Susa in early April and followed the shortest route, he must have arrived at Jerusalem in early June.

Upon arriving in Jerusalem, Nehemiah spent three days quietly observing his surroundings (2:11). No doubt he spent the greatest part of those three days in prayerful evaluation as he listened to the people's conversations, generally looked around the city, and assessed the spiritual atmosphere. During those three days, he told no one why he had come to Jerusalem. He needed a truly objective picture of things, and probably didn't want to create any momentum until he had an opportunity to formulate a plan.

7. Why is concerted prayer so important when a spiritual leader is assessing ministry needs?

8. Why might a spiritual leader skimp on the amount of prayer he puts into assessing needs?

9. What might be some consequences of implementing a plan before prayerfully assessing needs?

The work of God is the most important work on earth. It should be conducted as such. Do we dare engage in the work of God in a manner that is any less substantial than that which we would offer in our endeavors that are solely tied to this world? Nehemiah did not begin his task haphazardly. He undertook it with the utmost seriousness in his planning and preparation.

Nehemiah's Careful Assessment

Nehemiah's general understanding of the state of Jerusalem's walls and gates was insufficient for making a detailed reconstruction plan. He needed to make a more careful inspection. If he did that in broad daylight, however, he would arouse suspicion or at least curiosity. That being the case, he planned a nighttime inspection while most people were asleep. He selected a few trustworthy men to assist him and road on a sure-footed mule. At the established time, Nehemiah began inspecting the walls by moonlight (2:12, 13).

10. Why should leaders not base their plans on their assumptions about the needs?

11. When has a bad assumption derailed what you thought was a good plan?

Nehemiah began his inspection by exiting the old city through the valley gate on the west side, near "the dragon well" (2:13). Riding slowly, he proceeded southward along the outside of the wall until he came to the dung gate on the southern tip. The dung gate faced the Hinnom Valley. Here, Nehemiah stopped and carefully observed the ruins.

From the dung gate, he rode northward on the east side of the city until he came to the fountain gate and the king's pool (2:14). Piles of ruin and rubble blocked his progress at that point.

Verse 15 is difficult to interpret. Perhaps Nehemiah walked up the Kidron Valley for a short distance on foot and then returned. Or, perhaps he took a different path with his beast up the Kidron Valley and circled the northern sector of the city before returning to "the gate of the valley." Either of these possibilities is plausible. We can be sure that Nehemiah positioned himself so that he could see the entire length of the wall (2:15).

12. Reflect on Nehemiah's emotional response to the broken walls and burned gates. What do you think he felt?

13. What thoughts about God undoubtedly went through his mind as he surveyed the ruins?

14. How might a spiritual leader keep his emotions from allowing him to assess needs correctly?

Guarded Assessment

Nehemiah still needed a little more time to draw conclusions from what he observed and to forge a viable plan. He still did not tell the general public about his inspection of the walls (2:16). Also, he chose not to tell Jerusalem's religious leaders.

15. How might a skillful leader know when it is the appropriate time to launch a new endeavor?

MAKING IT PERSONAL

16. For what ministry tasks are you currently responsible? Which ones require careful assessment?

17. What project assessment questions do you need to ask? Add to the list below.
    - What needs to be done?
    - How much time will this project require?
    - What resources are necessary?
    - How much will it cost?

Nehemiah gives us a wonderful example of planning. He shows us that the process often requires hard work and diligence. Sadly, the work of God is sometimes done with little regard for wise planning, despite the many Scriptural admonitions on this subject (cf. Luke 14:28–30).

18. Ask God to help you carefully plan your service for Him.

Get to Work!

LESSON 5

Scripture Focus

Nehemiah 2:17–20

Theme

A spiritual leader motivates others to serve the Lord faithfully by encouraging them and teaching them to trust God.

Memory Verse

"Then answered [Nehemiah] them, and said unto them, The God of heaven, he will prosper us; therefore we his servants will arise and build" (Nehemiah 2:20a).

GETTING STARTED

On October 4th, 1957, scientists noticed that the frequency of the radio signals transmitted by Sputnik, a small Russian satellite, increased as it approached and decreased as it moved away. This was caused by the Doppler Effect. This meant they could track objects moving through space and that objects in space could pinpoint a signal coming from earth. This discovery was the genesis for today's GPS. Since that discovery, GPS has become so reliable that we take it for granted.

1. Describe your level of trust in the GPS driving directions in your car or from your phone.

2. How has your trust level changed over time?

Nehemiah called on his fellow repatriated Jews to tackle the enormous job of rebuilding the walls of Jerusalem. He pointed to God's good and sovereign hand as a primary motivator. God's hand is still good, sovereign, and trustworthy today. We ought to be just as motivated to serve God as Nehemiah was nearly 2,500 years ago.

SEARCHING THE SCRIPTURES

The work of God in Scripture is always connected to building. In our present age, church buildings are important to us. However, the most important building program on earth during the church age is entirely spiritual. It is the work of Christ in building His church (cf. Matt. 16:18). Passages such as 1 Corinthians 3:9, Ephesians 2:19–22, and 1 Peter 2:5 emphasize a spiritual building rather than physical buildings. In the Old Testament, though, the work of God often took on a physical nature. But even then, the purpose of the building projects in the Old Testament were to bring glory to God. Nehemiah understood that purpose as he motivated the repatriated Jews to join in rebuilding Jerusalem's walls.

Nehemiah Confronted the Need

We do not know how much time elapsed between the events recorded in verses 16 and 17. More than likely, the event recorded in verse 17 took place the day after Nehemiah's nighttime inspection of the ruined walls. At this point, Nehemiah faced as strong a challenge as he had when he approached the Persian king about returning to Judah. He needed to present his plan to all the people and motivate them to rebuild the walls. Exercising the authority God had given him, Nehemiah addressed the citizens of Jerusalem.

3. Read Nehemiah 2:17. Why do you think Nehemiah didn't spend a lot of time describing the plight of the city?

4. Nehemiah was wise not to dwell on the city's needs. What other precautions might a leader observe in communicating needs to potential volunteers?

Without a city wall, the Jews were defenseless against attack. Nehemiah's attitude in communicating that fact, however, was not one of self-righteous condemnation. He consistently used the pronouns "we" and "us." In fact, when speaking of the distress of the city, he boldly exclaimed, you "see the distress that *we* are in." By being up front with the people and by including himself as one of them, he was already winning the confidence of Jerusalem's population.

Nehemiah Shared His Vision

Having assessed Jerusalem's need firsthand and having drafted a plan, Nehemiah was ready to call the people to action. He appealed to the Jews with a confident challenge saying, "Come, and let *us* build up the wall of Jerusalem" (2:17). We might liken his encouragement to a coach who is addressing his winless football team before they face the nation's number one team. "We can do this if we work together and give our best!" The Jews, like a beleaguered football team, found hope in their leader's encouraging words.

5. How might a leader's passion and conviction affect your motivation to serve God?

6. Nehemiah 2:17b. What did Nehemiah give as the reason the people needed to build the city wall?

7. Whose reputation was on the line as the city sat in ruins?

The nations around Judah had different gods. Those gods were revered and respected according to the military successes of the nation. A nation filled with ruins tarnished her god's reputation. When the nations looked at Jerusalem, they didn't think very highly of Jehovah. Nehemiah wanted that to change not only to correct misconceptions about God, but also to provide the world with a beacon of hope. Jerusalem was the city of God. It was the mount of God's glory and "the joy of the whole earth" (Psalm 48:1, 2). Jerusalem needed to be built and strong in order to reflect God's holiness and power to the lost nations in the world.

8. Sometimes a ministry leader will motivate others to get involved in his ministry so he can make a name for himself. How successful do such endeavors end up being?

Nehemiah's Report about God's Faithfulness

As Nehemiah began his report of the events that led up to this pivotal moment, he assured the Jews that the hand of God was "good upon" him.

9. Read Nehemiah 2:18. Why do you think the people found the account of God's hand on Nehemiah's life so motivating?

The words, "the hand of my God which was good upon me," referred to both blessing and direction from God. Nehemiah's testimony showed that God had not forgotten His people. God once again proved He will always be faithful to His promises. Nehemiah's arrival was a sign of God's blessing.

10. Describe a time when seeing God's clear direction and provision motivated you to take part in a ministry.

Nehemiah's Report about the King's Favor

After Nehemiah told the Jews about God, his spiritual authority, he referenced his earthly authority, the king, and thereby kept his priorities in balance. The people no doubt marveled as Nehemiah told them of his royal position, the king's new decree, and the king's graciousness in providing Nehemiah with safe passage and the necessary timber (2:18).

Nehemiah must have explained the significance of his conversation with Artaxerxes I. The "captains of the army and horsemen" (2:9) around him would have been a visual aid of the kind of credibility that Nehemiah brought with him to this post.

While Nehemiah gave an honest report of the blessing of the Lord and his relationship with the king, he did not present himself as more important than anyone else. Within that context, the people quickly accepted Nehemiah's leadership and bought into his vision. They knew that under Nehemiah's leadership they had everything they needed to accomplish the task of rebuilding, and thus responded in unity, "Let us rise up and build" (2:18). The statement that follows: "So they strengthened their hands for this good work," may describe the people's immediate preparation to participate in the rebuilding project. However, it may mean they encouraged themselves for the good cause. In either case, Nehemiah certainly succeeded in motivating the people by encouraging them.

A foolish leader might have driven the people away at the very start and lost his opportunity to work with them. Nehemiah did not blame the people either for trying to rebuild the wall prematurely (cf. Ezra 4:12) or for presiding over its renewed destruction. Instead, he gave them a fresh start and a new opportunity to rebuild Jerusalem for the glory of God.

As we have seen, Nehemiah placed the emphasis on the group in his short but rousing speech. Nehemiah's courageous call to rebuild the city transformed them, and his vision became their vision.

11. What will happen to a leader's effectiveness if he does not take time to communicate his vision to those who will participate in the ministry?

Nehemiah's emphasis was on unity, teamwork, and cooperation. Nehemiah was the first one to make that emphasis clear and to foster an environment in which such a spirit could flourish. In this and other ways, Nehemiah offered an amazing contrast to the men who had previously attempted to lead the people in Jerusalem (cf. 5:15).

Nehemiah's Determination to Trust God

How a leader handles opposition can make or break the spirits of those who follow him. Just after Nehemiah delivered an encouraging motivational speech and the people responded positively, opposition arose. God used this opposition, however, as an opportunity for the Jews to observe Nehemiah under fire. Nehemiah's wise response to the opposition fortified the people's determination to rise up and build.

A third enemy surfaced in Jerusalem in alliance with Sanballat the Horonite and Tobiah the Ammonite. He was Geshem, the Arabian (Neh. 2:19). Geshem was a powerful king of Kedar. He ruled a league of Arabian tribes that controlled Moab, sections of Arabia, Edom, and borders of Egypt.

Sanballat, Tobiah, and Geshem quickly learned about Nehemiah's speech and plans. Perhaps a Jewish traitor had told them what Nehemiah had said, or perhaps they had been in the audience themselves.

As soon as the three enemies learned what Nehemiah intended to do, they laughed mockingly.

12. Read Nehemiah 2:19. What makes mocking laughter such a powerful attack against leaders?

The three enemies "despised" the Jews and falsely accused Nehemiah. They asked him if he would rebel against the king. Perhaps they wanted to frighten the Jews by suggesting that the king would consider their action. Such opposition was a preview of that which was to come during the actual building of the wall (Neh. 4—6). Nehemiah responded courageously when it was most crucial for all to see.

13. Read Nehemiah 2:20. What did Nehemiah's answer reveal about where his confidence came from?

Nehemiah's reply, "The God of heaven, he will prosper us" (2:20), both silenced the critics and encouraged the Jews. Not only did Nehemiah use a name for God that was familiar in the Persian Empire, but he also used a title that strongly asserted the sovereignty of God. Perhaps in the use of this title, Nehemiah was reminding his opposition that God sees the difference between truth and error. In any event, He believed the work could not be thwarted if the builders trusted in Him.

Nehemiah's Determination to Serve God

Nehemiah's second statement in verse 20 demonstrated his character. He declared, "We his servants will arise and build." Again, he stated his absolute resolve. For Nehemiah, this project was a commitment to serve God and restore His great name.

14. Read Galatians 6:9 and 1 Corinthians 15:58. What reasons do believers have for continuing to serve God despite opposition?

By telling the adversaries they had "no portion," Nehemiah reminded them that they were not Jews. They did not share in the rich heritage of Jerusalem. In stating that they had "no right," he meant they had no legal authority over Jerusalem. Artaxerxes I had just appointed him the temporary governor of Jerusalem, and so this matter of the city's rebuilding was none of their concern.

By saying the opposition had "no memorial," Nehemiah may have been referring to their different religious systems, or he may have been telling them that they would not go down in Judah's own history. If this is the case, Nehemiah frankly told them that they had no past, present, or future ties with Jerusalem.

As in Nehemiah's day, completing God's work is not easy. We face the forces of overt evil from the outside and apathy and apostasy from within. But if we focus on God's greatness rather than on the enormity of the task, we will see Him do great things through us for the sake of His name.

MAKING IT PERSONAL

15. What are some ways you could motivate those you lead?

16. Why is encouragement a particularly effective means of motivating them?

17. Who will you encourage to serve the Lord?

Delegate!

Scripture Focus

Nehemiah 3

Theme

A spiritual leader delegates tasks to responsible workers.

Memory Verse

"So built we the wall; and all the wall was joined together unto the half thereof: for the people had a mind to work" (Nehemiah 4:6).

GETTING STARTED

What do glory hogs, perfectionists, and control freaks all have in common? They all have a hard time delegating responsibility to other people. They want to control both the process and the outcome. If you are one of those types of people, then you completely understand!

1. Would you rather work on a project with other people or alone? What is the reason for your choice?

2. Is one approach better than the other? Explain.

Nehemiah organized his workers and delegated work for them to do. He counted on all of them to do their job well.

Delegation is an important practice for leaders. Those leaders who try to do all the work themselves will not realize success. Nehemiah is a good example of the benefits of delegation.

SEARCHING THE SCRIPTURES

Having successfully recruited the people of Jerusalem to rebuild the city's walls, Nehemiah needed to organize the workers and the work. Chapter 3 of Nehemiah explains how he did this.

At first glance one might be tempted to skip over Nehemiah 3 entirely. Like the genealogical sections we find at various places in the Bible, this chapter is largely a list of names. We might wonder how it could possibly have any relation to us today.

To find the value of this chapter, do not try to attach spiritual or hidden meanings to the names of these gates. As many have noted, this type of effort may be an exercise in the power of imagination, but it is not an exercise in proper Biblical interpretation.

We can gleam some principles for delegating from Nehemiah's examples and from the specific notes he included about the work and the workers. Those principles form the outline for this lesson.

We should also recognize that this chapter is the very crux of the book of Nehemiah. It presents the 52 days of rebuilding the walls of Jerusalem (cf. 6:15). Writing by inspiration of the Spirit of God, Nehemiah chose to make this account more detail-oriented than action-oriented. It nevertheless gives the template for understanding the action contained in the rest of the book, including the opposition the people encountered in chapter 4, the internal financial strife the people faced in chapter 5, the subtle scheming that Nehemiah had to overcome in chapter 6, or the final victory that was celebrated when the building was finished (6:15). The entire second half of the book (7—13) takes place in the context of the city and the walls.

The rebuilt wall was about 2.5 miles long. Every person who worked on that amazing wall was important to God. He recorded the results of their efforts for us in His inspired Word. There could be no higher praise for them than that.

Delegate Work with People's Interests in Mind

In explaining how he organized the rebuilding effort, Nehemiah began with the northern wall and moved counterclockwise around the city of Jerusalem. The Sheep Gate and the Fish Gate, with the towers of Meah and Hananeel between them, were located on the northern wall.

Wisely, Nehemiah delegated work according to the interests of the workers, putting them where they would be the most concerned and hence the most productive. Perhaps the prime example of this concept is listed first. When Eliashib, the high priest, and the other temple priests volunteered to work, Nehemiah gave them the assignment of rebuilding the Sheep Gate (Neh. 3:1). They accepted this assignment seriously as a part of their sacred function, and therefore "sanctified" the Sheep Gate for the Lord.

The Sheep Gate was important because of its relationship to the nearby temple. Sheep were purchased at the Sheep Gate, not only for personal use, but also for use as sacrifices on the temple altar. These sacrifices provided ceremonial cleansing for the faithful Jews.

3. Why is it wise to delegate work to believers according to their spiritual interests?

Delegate Work with an Understanding of the People

The rebuilding of the wall progressed from gate to gate, and it included the gates themselves. This undertaking required an equal distribution of the work force throughout the city. Nehemiah not only assigned certain people to certain tasks but also placed them where he believed their work would be the most effective (3:2). His master plan demonstrated both an understanding of the project and a familiarity with the people.

Nehemiah's organizational skills are manifested in many subtle details of this chapter. We find words like "next unto," or something similar, many times in this chapter. Those words are a clue that Nehemiah was concerned that the members of his team fit together as they worked side by side. They also indicate that he emphasized their cooperation one with another.

4. What does it take for leaders to become familiar with their workers?

The situation in Jerusalem reminds us of the interdependent relationship that members of the church body have with one another as they serve together to fulfill God's mission (cf. 1 Cor. 12:12–26). In both cases, every member is important. Nehemiah's team could not afford for even one member of the wall-building team to be absent or to let down his or her fellow workers. Their lives, the security of the entire city, and, most importantly, God's name and reputation were on the line.

Delegate Work to Willing People

Nehemiah's next description of the rebuilding effort focuses on the westward section the northern wall to the Fish Gate (3:3), the location of Jerusalem's fish market. There Nehemiah observed that the Tekoites worked without the assistance of "their nobles" (3:4, 5). These Tekoites represented large groups of workers from outlying regions of Judah. Perhaps these nobles thought they were too important to perform such a menial task.

5. What do people with superiority complexes do to the morale of a group of workers?

No leader can expect to recruit every available person for a Christian service project. Nevertheless, Nehemiah refused to become discouraged. He simply continued to delegate the work to those who were willing to get involved.

The Tekoites performed double work (3:27). Perhaps they were driven by the shame of their own officials. No doubt they were inspired by Nehemiah's method of handling the situation.

6. Who ends up losing the most when some workers think they are too privileged to work?

Nehemiah 3:6–13 describes the rebuilding of the western sections of the wall. Both the Old Gate (3:6) and Valley Gate (3:13) were on this wall. The Old Gate was probably the Gate to the oldest section of the city.

Note that Shallum's *daughters* helped with the repairs (3:12). Obviously, Nehemiah used all the people who were willing to work, giving them meaningful jobs they could handle.

7. What might leaders communicate to their people if they recruit only the best, brightest, or strongest to complete projects?

Delegate Work with Clear Instructions

Overlooking the Tyropoeon Valley on the west side of Jerusalem was the Valley Gate (3:13). This was the first gate Nehemiah rode through on his nighttime inspection of the walls (cf. Neh. 2:9–16). When Nehemiah delegated the work here and other places, he gave specific instructions. He told Hanun and the inhabitants of Zanoah exactly what to do. He said to repair the doors, locks, bars, and one thousand cubits of the wall southward. Good leaders give specific instructions. In addition, a clear job description removes uncertainty, anxiety, and confusion.

8. Describe a time when you wasted time by either not giving clear instructions or not receiving clear instructions.

Delegate Unpleasant Work with Care

On the southern tip of the old city of Jerusalem stood the Dung Gate (3:14). Jerusalem's garbage was carried out of the city through the Dung Gate and tossed into the Hinnom Valley below. Fires were kept burning around the clock to consume the city's refuse. The task of rebuilding the Dung Gate would have been extremely unpleasant. Workers would contend with the smell of burning garbage and the reputation of that gate. They had to complete the job, though, to secure Jerusalem's defensive system. Nehemiah boldly assigned this task to Malchiah, the son of Rechab (3:14). An effective leader must assign unpleasant tasks as well as pleasant ones, for every necessary task is important in God's work.

Delegate Work with a Goal of Excellence

Ironically, not far away from the Dung Gate and pleasantly located was the Fountain Gate. It faced the Kidron Valley, which extended northward from the Hinnom Valley at Jerusalem's southeast corner.

A path through this gate stretched southward to En Rogel, one of just two fresh water sources for the city. It also opened the city to the cool refreshing Pool of the King's Garden.

Near the Fountain Gate, Nehemiah wanted to restore some of the old city's original beauty and splendor. He assigned workers to restore the pool's walls and the stone stairway that descended into the royal gardens of the Kidron (3:15, 16).

A successful leader is driven to excellence. He is not content doing simply what is required; he motivates people to do the best possible job to the glory of God.

9. How might you respond to a leader who places little emphasis on the quality of your work?

Delegate Difficult Work to Earnest Workers

Along the eastern portion of the wall stood the remaining four gates: the Water Gate, Horse Gate, Eastern Gate, and the Miphkad Gate (3:26, 27). Evidently these gates didn't need repairs, but the walls connecting them required much work.

The people of Jerusalem passed through the Water Gate on their way to procure water from the Gihon Spring, Jerusalem's second supply of fresh water. The walls around the gate encompassed a sizable public square that needed restored. The challenge of restoring the public square was greater than most of the others, and therefore required highly motivated workers. Nehemiah wisely recruited Baruch, the son of Zabbai, to lead this project. He did his work "earnestly" (3:20).

10. What could happen to a worker who lacks the earnestness or skills to handle a difficult task?

Delegate Work to Those with Vested Interests

The Horse Gate stood at the easternmost point of the city facing the Kidron Valley. Biblical scholars believe this gate was used for palace traffic. It was therefore viewed as the royal entrance to the city, and probably used for official business. This would have made the Horse Gate a central target during military attack.

Demonstrating wise insight, Nehemiah delegated those who lived around this area to work on their own walls (3:28). By asking them to work on their own defense system, he appealed to their sense of vulnerability, knowing that such motivation would assist them in completing the task at hand. Like Nehemiah, good leaders use the motivation of vested interest.

11. Why do workers with a vested interest in the task provide an advantage for a leader?

Because the Eastern Gate led to the Temple area, it was known as the sacred gate (3:29). Because of its eastern exposure and proximity to the Horse Gate, Nehemiah continued to delegate the work to those whose houses were nearby (3:30).

The Eastern Gate may be the only gate that is today close to its original location. Ezekiel prophesied that the Son of Man would pass through this gate, and later it would be sealed shut (Ezek. 44:1, 2). Jesus passed through this gate during His triumphal entry into Jerusalem. Later, in 1543, the Eastern Gate was sealed shut for good by Sultan Sulieman.

The so-called Miphkad Gate probably served as either an inspection station for travelers entering Jerusalem, or as a civil garrison for either justice officials or military personnel (Neh. 3:31). This would have been a logical spot for vendors to market their wares. Perhaps for that reason, Nehemiah insightfully used merchants and goldsmiths to rebuild the adjacent walls. This would have been their marketplace (3:32). As a skilled leader, Nehemiah made use of the professional interests of the people.

There are 38 individuals representing 42 different groups of people listed in Nehemiah 3. History knows almost nothing of most of these people, including their identities. Yet they are known to God. He recorded their heroic deeds in this amazing chapter. The focus of this chapter is on these individuals, not just their numbers or the results of their labors that can be quantified.

MAKING IT PERSONAL

12. Which of the delegation principles (listed as the subtitles for this lesson) speak to a situation in your life?

13. Which ones do you need to work on implementing?

14. Why might leaders fail to delegate?

15. What are some of the consequences of failing to delegate responsibilities?

Facing Opposition

LESSON 7

Scripture Focus

Nehemiah 4:1—6:14

Theme

A spiritual leader handles opposition with direction from and dependence on God.

Memory Verse

"Also I said, It is not good that ye do: ought ye not to walk in the fear of our God because of the reproach of the heathen our enemies?" (Nehemiah 5:9).

GETTING STARTED

"He has a right to criticize, who has a heart to help." So said Abraham Lincoln.

Unfortunately, most critics have a heart to hurt. Their criticism and opposition of others comes from a desire to tear people down, especially successful people.

Critics are attracted to successful people. They to love to find an angle from which to hurl criticism. So, responding appropriately to critics and opposition should become our focus. Doing away with our opposition is impossible!

1. Do you think Christians receive more criticism from non-Christians or from fellow Christians? Why?

2. Why are Christians sometimes criticized in their work for the Lord?

Receiving criticism for serving God is not easy to do, especially when we are serving sacrificially. The Jews and Nehemiah faced criticism, but their desire to please God kept them on task. Nehemiah is an excellent example for leaders today.

SEARCHING THE SCRIPTURES

A servant of God cannot avoid opposition, so he must be prepared to respond to it in a godly manner. Nehemiah 4:1–6:14 describes four episodes of opposition that challenged Nehemiah's rebuilding effort. Nehemiah handled each episode in exemplary ways.

Threat: Ridiculing Enemies

When Sanballat heard about the Jews' progress in rebuilding Jerusalem, he was enraged. He expressed his rage in ridicule and mockery (4:1).

As governor of Samaria, Sanballat felt threatened by the prospect of a restructured Jerusalem. He abhorred the thought of Jerusalem regaining a place of influence near his realm. A Jewish influence would mean economic distress for Samaria since the trade routes of the day would go back through Jerusalem instead of through his land.

Anger is often rooted in jealousy, fear, or pride. Destructive criticism is normally rooted in anger. Sanballat's ridicule of Nehemiah must have sprung from jealousy. The word "wroth" (4:1) carries the idea of burning.

3. What sinful reactions might we have when someone becomes jealously angry with us?

Sanballat had already accused the Jews of rebelling against Artaxerxes I (Neh. 2:19). He changed his method to mock the Jews' efforts, intimating that they would never be able to finish the monumental project (4:2). Tobiah the Ammonite agreed and hurled intense personal attacks on the Jews (4:3).

4. Read Nehemiah 4:2, 3. What was Tobiah's ridiculous personal attack on the Jews?

5. Why might personal attacks be so effective in getting believers distracted from completing their tasks?

Response: Prayer and Determination

Nehemiah responded to Sanballat and Tobiah's ridicule with godly wisdom. He immediately prayed, calling upon God's sense of justice (4:4). His prayer aligned with God's promises in the Abrahamic Covenant. In the Covenant, God promised to bless those who bless Abraham's descendants but to curse those who curse them (Gen. 12:3). Of course, Nehemiah could count on God to remain faithful to His promises.

6. Was Nehemiah's response a sign of weakness or strength? Explain.

Nehemiah met ridicule with prayer and then led the people to work with greater determination (Neh. 4:6). Obviously, his determination positively affected God's people. His example should encourage us too.

Threat: Discouraged Workers

Sanballat and Tobiah's anger spread to neighboring regions so that the Jews faced opposition from every side: the Samaritans in the north, the Ammonites in the east, the Arabs in the south, and the Ashdodites in the west.

The enemies were "wroth," meaning they burned with anger (4:7). They conspired to attack Jerusalem in hopes the workers would be spooked and quit (4:8). Once again Nehemiah responded with prayerful determination (4:9). The tense for the verb "prayed" indicates the prayer was intense.

Nehemiah's workers felt vulnerable while working hard under the threat of an enemy attack. Soon they became discouraged. To ease their fears, Nehemiah used some of the workers to set a guard around the city, but that meant those still working had to shoulder a heavier load. The workers grew physically and emotionally weary and lost their perspective (4:10). Suddenly the rubbish seemed more imposing than the wall did impressive. In their discouragement, the people of Judah began advancing the message of their adversaries (4:11, 12).

7. Read Nehemiah 4:10–12. What might have happened if Nehemiah had grown frustrated with his workers, ignored their discouragement, and told them to get back to work?

We may lose our perspective too when we are physically and emotionally weary. In such cases, it is wise to refresh both body and spirit as much as necessary before pressing ahead. A wise leader will recognize the potential for discouragement to set in.

Response: Faith and Strategy

Nehemiah took to heart the discouragement of his people, and he took seriously the military threat. He responded with faith and strategy as he kept the people's focus on the task of building the wall. After carefully setting the people in order, he spoke words of encouragement (4:13, 14). As a result, the enemies were discouraged, realizing that their plans had been exposed and defeated while God's people were energized to build (4:15).

To protect the work, Nehemiah appointed half of the people to work while the other half served as guards (4:16–18). Ranking officials stayed at the rear. Builders who transported materials carried their supplies in one hand and a weapon in the other. Every worker kept on building, with a sword by his side. Nehemiah also kept beside him day and night a trumpeter who would sound an alert if necessary (4:18–20). These measures still put high demands on everyone, but Nehemiah's words encouraged the workers to accept the new normal and step up their efforts.

8. Read Nehemiah 4:20. What gave Nehemiah and the workers confidence as they labored in a dangerous environment?

Nehemiah's strategy wasn't a substitute for divine assistance. He anchored his faith in the Lord (4:20). He balanced trust in God's sovereignty with recognition of human responsibility. He was responsible to develop a comprehensive strategy for the defense of the city that allowed for continuing progress. In the process, he overwhelmed and disheartened the enemy.

Nehemiah's workers responded well. They labored hard, making use of every moment of daylight (4:21). To protect the people and the city, everyone slept in Jerusalem, fully clothed and ready for battle (4:22, 23).

Threat: Greedy Jews

After conquering external opposition, Nehemiah encountered internal conflict. The Bible often points out the reality that the main hindrance to progress in the work of God is the spiritual condition and actions of His people.

9. Is conflict among believers more difficult to cope with than conflict between believers and unbelievers? Explain.

After a period of working and guarding the city, Jerusalem suddenly evidenced low morale. Note the contrast from the previous chapter: "The work is great" (4:19), and "There was a great cry of the people and of their wives against their brethren the Jews" (5:1). The people were fighting amongst themselves. The conflict was so intense that Nehemiah had to suspend building temporarily to deal with the difficulties. The motivation to rebuild the walls was temporarily forgotten under the weight of the circumstances. The work of God always suffers when His people lose their sense of purpose and unity and instead focus on problems of their own making.

10. When have you witnessed the work of a church halting under the weight of internal conflict?

The atmosphere in the city was emotionally charged. Verse 2 gives the reason: Jerusalem's food supply was running low. Apparently failed crops, perhaps due to a lack of attention being given to agricultural efforts, had caused a famine. If that were not bad enough, the city had taken on the responsibility of feeding the workers who had come from all parts of Judah.

11. Read Nehemiah 5:2–5. How would you describe the Jews' treatment of each other?

Those who had food were selling it for a large profit, taking advantage of the situation. These exorbitant prices drove some Jerusalem dwellers to mortgage their properties (5:3). Others were forced to borrow to pay the heavy taxes to the Persian Empire (5:4). To make matters worse, they had to pay high interest rates to Jewish lenders (5:3, 4). Some Jewish families even had to sell their children into slavery to pay these high costs of living (5:5).

Response: Confrontation and Restitution

Nehemiah became angry when he heard the cry of the people and received these reports (5:6).

12. What words in this verse show that Nehemiah was using self-control in dealing with the Jew's gross mistreatment of each other?

Nehemiah challenged the people to fear God and held every offender accountable (5:7b–10). He settled for nothing less than complete restitution. Mortgaged lands would be returned along with interest (5:11).

Nobles had to take an oath that they would do exactly what Nehemiah had outlined and repay the money (5:11–13). Nehemiah even gave them an object lesson by shaking out his clothing, picturing what the Lord would do to those who went back on their word to correct the situation. Nehemiah also wanted the people to consider their testimony before pagans, who could clearly see that some were putting personal profit ahead of the work of God.

With candor and pure motive, Nehemiah pointed to his own behavior as a better example to the people (5:14–18; cf. 1 Cor. 9:15). He shared with the people how he never misused his own office as governor for personal gain. On the contrary, he sought to constantly use his authority for the good of others. More than 150 Jews were treated to meals at Nehemiah's own table during those lean days (5:17). At the same time, he recommitted to completing the wall project (5:16).

Nehemiah could appropriately ask the people of Jerusalem to do as he had done. When a person lives according to Biblical principles, he can exercise valid leadership and confront sin!

Nehemiah closed the chapter with a variation on his favorite prayer (5:19).

Chapter 5 teaches us that the greatest potential for hindering the work of God is found within God's people themselves. The risk is even greater when His servants have just come through a period of victory and find themselves exhausted from strenuous effort.

Threat: Plotting Enemies

Having overcome internal strife, the people were now stronger than ever. The only task that remained was the placing of the gates. Sanballat, Tobiah, and Geshem were furious at this progress. Still hoping to thwart the completion of the project, they launched desperate attacks on Nehemiah.

First, Nehemiah's enemies tried to lure him to the plain of Ono, about 20 miles northwest of Jerusalem, for discussions. This set-up would have taken him away from his work and given them an opportunity to assassinate him. They requested such a meeting on four occasions (6:1, 2, 4–7). Nehemiah understood that it is never possible to compromise with the enemies of God in a manner that will please God.

Next came the most diabolical plot of all. The enemies of God had Sanballat's servant hand Nehemiah an unsealed letter. It alleged that Nehemiah was attempting to establish himself as Judah's king (6:6, 7a). They had the gall to pose as Nehemiah's friends, offering to help him out of the predicament they had created (6:7b).

13. Why should we not be surprised that Nehemiah's enemies used lies and deception to try to halt the completion of Jerusalem's wall?

Finally, Nehemiah's enemies sought to discredit him. They enlisted the aid of Shemaiah, a person Nehemiah apparently trusted, to lure him into the temple. Shemaiah was to tell Nehemiah of would-be-assassins in the city and invite him to take shelter in the temple (6:10). If Nehemiah had heeded Shemaiah's advice, he would have violated the law of God, for only priests were authorized to enter the holy place (cf. 6:13). Such an action would have discredited Nehemiah in the eyes of both God and men.

The enemies of God never rest. What they cannot accomplish through conflict, they will often attempt to do through compromise or conspiracy. Nehemiah provides an example of how to handle such diversions.

Response: Integrity and Firmness

When the enemies tried to lure Nehemiah to the plain of Ono, Nehemiah saw through their scheme. He simply refused to go, and honestly told them the work would suffer without his supervision (6:3).

After receiving the fictitious letter, Nehemiah forthrightly denied any aspirations to be Judah's king, and he rebuked the enemies for forging such a report (6:8). At that point, Nehemiah boldly prayed once again.

14. Read Nehemiah 6:9. What did Nehemiah ask God to do for him as he faced personal attacks from his enemies?

Shemaiah counseled Nehemiah to disobey the law (6:10). While his words, at first glance, appeared to be wise, they were completely unbiblical. This alerted Nehemiah to the fact that this was neither a true prophecy nor good advice. Nehemiah understood that the law of God forbade non-priests to enter the temple on penalty of death (cf. Num. 1:51; 3:10; 18:3–7). Nehemiah saw through the deceptive plan to ruin his testimony, and his unquestioned obedience to God's revealed Word saved him from both God's judgment and the enemy's machinations.

15. Why is remaining blameless so important for a leader as he faces opposition?

MAKING IT PERSONAL

16. How have you responded to opposition as you have served God?

17. What might God think of your responses?

18. Critics are sure to come if you are engaged in successfully building the work of God. Ask God to strengthen your hands as opposition tries to pull you from God's will.

Give God the Glory

Scripture Focus

Nehemiah 6:15–19

Theme

A spiritual leader directs glory to God for tasks successfully completed.

Memory Verses

"And whatsoever ye do, do it heartily, as to the Lord, and not unto men; knowing that of the Lord ye shall receive the reward of the inheritance: for ye serve the Lord Christ" (Colossians 3:23, 24).

GETTING STARTED

When the Jews finished the walls under Nehemiah's leadership in just fifty-two days, they created a wow factor. But they directed the wow at God rather than themselves.

1. What amazing things have you seen God accomplish through people faithfully serving Him?

2. Who got the glory for the accomplishments?

God wants to do great things through us too. When He does, we need to make sure He gets the credit even when we want to jump up and down and draw all the attention to ourselves.

SEARCHING THE SCRIPTURES

When Nehemiah faced threats, false accusations, and slander from his enemies, he chose to trust in the Lord rather than acting hastily out of fear. In Nehemiah 6:10–14, Nehemiah saved his life by obeying God and remaining in the place of danger rather than following man's wisdom and seeking his own comfort and safety.

Under the magnificent leadership of Nehemiah, Jewish cupbearer to King Artaxerxes I, the city of Jerusalem had finally been restored. Ever since Nebuchadnezzar's Babylonian invasion of August 9, 586 BC, the city's walls and gates had been in a state of ruin. Although the temple had been rebuilt under the supervision of Zerubbabel and rededicated in 516 BC, the city's walls and gates remained in disrepair. The repatriated Jews at one point started the work but abandoned it when the king ordered it halted and their enemies tore down and burned the progress they had made. King Artaxerxes I eventually reversed his decree, prompted by the explanation and appeal of Nehemiah. The king even donated wood for the project from his own forest.

Jerusalem's population worked and completed the restoration of the walls ahead of schedule. The completion came more than 90 years after Zerubbabel returned to Jerusalem in 538 BC with the first wave of Jews.

Nehemiah provided the organizational plan and delegation of forces. The project included 14,000 feet of wall. Six gates received major repairs. All of this occurred during days of famine and military threat from all of Jerusalem's surrounding regions. When asked about his accomplishment, Nehemiah merely said in essence, "God did it!"

The Builders Completed the Wall

The building project was completed "in the twenty and fifth day of the month Elul" (Neh. 6:15). Some sources identify this day as the 3rd of September. The implication is striking. If the people finished the project at the end of Israel's summer, the workers must have labored through the hottest months of the year while carrying the extra weight of military weapons. Yet, Nehemiah neither gloated over the success nor tried to solicit any praise or credit. A spiritual leader does not seek credit for tasks accomplished in the strength of the Lord. His desire is to defer all glory to God.

3. Read Galatians 6:14. What did Paul say about boasting?

4. Why is the cross of Christ a good reminder of the foolishness of boasting about ourselves?

5. What has God done through your life that should cause you to give Him glory?

Nehemiah further reported that the entire rebuilding process took just fifty-two working days. Understanding that Jews did not work on the Sabbaths, we realize this feat was accomplished in less than nine weeks. Likely, the military threat had encouraged the people to work as fast as they could; nevertheless, they could not have accomplished their task without God's enabling help.

Nehemiah's words almost seem matter of fact as he states, "So the wall was finished" (6:15; cf. 4:6). Perhaps Nehemiah purposely avoided any appearance of self-glory over the accomplishment.

It is a privilege to be able to serve God with our talents and efforts. When we do so, He uses our service to mature us and to bring glory to Himself.

6. Since God deserves the glory for the work He does through us, does that mean we should never publicly or even privately acknowledge people for their work for the Lord? Explain.

Everyone who saw the repaired walls realized that the Lord had provided the authority for the rebuilding of this city. Since the opposition to this project was so great, God received even more glory from its completion. This could only be true, however, as Nehemiah's team abided by God's wisdom, plan, and methods.

7. How might we know if we are serving God for His glory?

The Builders Glorified God

8. Read Nehemiah 6:16. How did the Jews' enemies react to the completion of the walls?

None of the enemies' attempts to thwart the Jews' work had succeeded. The enemies never dreamed the repatriated Jews would see the enormous task through to the end. They had to be concerned about what else the Jews might accomplish through their God.

Jerusalem's enemies knew why they were defeated. They perceived that this work was made possible by God. Like so many today who know they are fighting a losing battle against God and continue to oppose His work, Jerusalem's enemies kept on opposing God's servant, Nehemiah.

Along with the perception that God had blessed His people, Jerusalem's enemies stood in awe of Him. Reluctantly, they also developed some respect for the Jews while their opinions of themselves must have dropped.

9. How do believers show that their work is of the Lord? What are the clues?

10. What do those who are willing to take on challenging work believe about God's abilities and desires?

The Opposition Persisted

The enemies of God neither easily give up nor worry about engaging in a fair fight.

11. Evaluate this statement: A great work for the Lord always attracts critics and enemies who try to undermine it.

Nehemiah 6:17–19 offers a key to understanding much of the opposition that Nehemiah and his builders faced in chapters four through six. The opposition stemmed from two compromising relationships in the life of Tobiah, the Ammonite leader (2:19).

Strange as it may seem, many people in Jerusalem were loyal to Tobiah, an avowed opponent of the work. Tobiah had numerous friends in Jerusalem, and he exchanged many letters with Judah's nobles (6:17).

Verse 18 sheds light on Tobiah's strong influence: "He was the son in law of Shechaniah the son of Arah," and his daughter-in-law was "the daughter of Meshullam the son of Berechiah." Thus, he was doubly connected to "the nobles of Judah" through these mixed marriages. Somehow these family connections gave Tobiah an introduction to the Judean nobles.

Both the law of Moses and Ezra's sermons (cf. Ezra 9, 10; cf. Neh. 10:30) prohibited the Jews from intermarrying with pagans to guard against pagan influence. Tobiah's relationships with Jews through marriage certainly gave him a foothold among the people of Jerusalem and an in with the nobles. The nobles connected to Tobiah were schemers who were attempting to play the leadership of Nehemiah and Tobiah off each other, desiring to manipulate circumstances to their advantage. This arrangement compromised Meshullam, who was one of Nehemiah's most dedicated workers (3:4, 30). Even "Eliashib the priest . . . was allied unto Tobiah" (13:4; cf. 13:7).

Tobiah's supporters gave Nehemiah many good reports about Tobiah (6:19). They also carried back to Tobiah everything that Nehemiah said about him. This was a most unhealthy "grapevine."

12. What could happen to a leader's work if he tries to track down and silence every unhealthy grapevine?

13. What is a better way to handle unhealthy grapevines?

This information about Tobiah's family relationships reveals how some of the people of Judah would have heard and then shared the message of discouragement that came from the enemies of Jerusalem in Nehemiah 4:10–12. At least a portion of them were under the influence of Tobiah. Doubtless they were worn down by his negative predictions. We can only infer that some people on Nehemiah's team may have been working covertly to spread the message of Tobiah through the ranks. The former would have been an issue of incompetence; the latter a matter of evil.

The New Testament addresses sins of slanderers or busybodies (1 Tim. 3:11; 5:12). People who engage in such sins can do immeasurable harm.

The Jews who opposed Nehemiah were foolish. If their alliance with Tobiah had succeeded, they would not necessarily have been protected or prosperous as a result. Tobiah didn't have their best interests at heart. They were, in fact, playing a dangerous game.

The Opposition Attacked

God used Nehemiah to bless Jerusalem, yet some of the people pushed him aside for the sake of Tobiah, an envious leader of lesser character. Nehemiah, however, refused to be intimidated by Tobiah's threatening letters (6:19). He continued to keep his focus on the glory of God.

14. Why might proud leaders try to placate their critics?

15. Read Galatians 1:10. What keeps a believer's focus on serving for the glory of God?

Despite Nehemiah's opposition, the initial work on the wall was finally finished. Doubtless, Nehemiah could envision this wall in his mind when he circled the ruins in the middle of the night after arriving in the land (2:12–16).

In our day, the work of building the church is no less daunting than was the task of rebuilding the walls of Jerusalem in Nehemiah's day. Christ said in Matthew 16:18 that we would face "the gates of hell" in working with Him in this endeavor. May God give us, and make us into, leaders like Nehemiah—full of courage and wisdom—who are up to this task.

MAKING IT PERSONAL

16. When has someone perceived God's work in your life?

17. How did that person respond?

18. What difficult tasks might God want you to tackle on His behalf? Start a neighborhood Bible study, witness to a family member, or take a short-term mission trip?

19. What truths about God should cause you to be willing to tackle difficult tasks?

20. What can you do to build your faith in God's ability to work in and through you to accomplish great things?

Act Wisely!

Scripture Focus

Nehemiah 7

Theme

A spiritual leader makes wise decisions.

Memory Verses

"See then that ye walk circumspectly, not as fools, but as wise, redeeming the time, because the days are evil. Wherefore be ye not unwise, but understanding what the will of the Lord is" (Ephesians 5:15–17).

GETTING STARTED

"Decisions, decisions, decisions!" For some people, that is a cry of frustration. Such people don't like making decisions. Decisions stress them out. For other people, it is a statement of anticipation. They love having the power to make all the decisions.

Personality has a lot to do with determining how we view decisions. But no matter our outlook or personality, decisions are part of our lives and part of being a leader.

1. Do you like being the decision maker in a group? Why?

2. Why does wanting to make all the decisions not necessarily make a person a good decision maker?

Nehemiah was God's decision maker in the newly walled Jerusalem. His decisions were wise and indicators of his close relationship with God.

SEARCHING THE SCRIPTURES

Nehemiah didn't pack up and return to Susa when the walls and gates were finished. He knew that there was still much to do. Jerusalem needed its own strong, local leadership. It needed an adequate plan of protection to maximize the use of the rebuilt walls. It needed to be repopulated with some of the people still living in other parts of Judah. It needed an equitable distribution of population. As a wise leader, Nehemiah looked beyond the immediate task to the process of follow-up.

It is always important to focus on protecting that which we have built up for the Lord, not for selfish reasons, but so that the glory of God and the value of works done for Him may be magnified and multiplied for the sake of eternity.

The focus of Nehemiah 7 is on the people who would literally fill the rebuilt city both for their own protection and to reinforce it against its enemies.

Nehemiah Wisely Appointed Hanani as a Leader

Now that the walls were rebuilt, the people of Jerusalem needed to post some guards. Nehemiah used his authority well. He appointed "porters" or gatekeepers to stand watch at the temple entrances and at the newly restored gates around the city wall (7:1). He also appointed singers and Levites. Perhaps these singers and Levites were supposed to assist the security force. On the other hand, Nehemiah may have appointed them to reinstitute a refurbished program of public worship. Singers did lead the daily worship services, and Levites functioned primarily as teachers of the law of God. Even if they simply assisted in the watch around the city, their constant presence would have reminded the people to worship God.

Nehemiah also recognized the need to appoint local leadership for Jerusalem. Perhaps the day-to-day details of city management were growing too large for him to handle by himself. In any event, the day would come when he would return to Susa. To leave the city well intact, it had to be self-governing.

3. How might your church's leaders build a strong leadership base for the church's future needs?

Nehemiah focused on appointing godly, qualified leadership (7:2). The first man Nehemiah appointed to help govern Jerusalem was his brother Hanani (1:2). This decision may appear to have been unwise, for Nehemiah risked being accused of nepotism (establishing a family powerbase). On the other hand, this selection showed much wisdom. Hanani and Nehemiah shared the same upbringing, training, ideals, values, and commitments. Hanani would certainly remain loyal to Nehemiah and resist the overtures of Tobiah's followers. Furthermore, Hanani had already proven himself as a loyal son of Judah. In fact, back in Persia he had given Nehemiah the initial report of Jerusalem's sad state. He was obviously a man the people could trust.

4. What do you think about appointing unfaithful, spiritually floundering people to leadership positions in order to challenge them to become strong, godly leaders?

5. What potential problems might come from such a decision?

Nehemiah Wisely Appointed Hananiah as a Leader

Probably because Hanani was Nehemiah's brother, Nehemiah appointed Hananiah as a second ruler (7:2). This appointment put to rest any fears of nepotism and added the benefit of additional manpower to handle all the details of city management. Hananiah was an experienced leader; he had already been serving as the "ruler of the palace." He impressed Nehemiah, however, for more reasons than just his experience.

6. Read Nehemiah 7:2. What qualities made Hananiah a good candidate for a leadership position?

7. Why would a fear of God be particularly important for Hananiah as he dealt with enemies both inside and outside Jerusalem?

8. Read Acts 6:1–7. What criteria were used to select the leaders in the early church?

9. How do these criteria compare with those Nehemiah used in appointing Hanani and Hananiah?

Hananiah did not know that Nehemiah was observing him as he faithfully fulfilled his daily tasks. Yet, because of his faithfulness, he became a co-ruler over all Jerusalem. When we are faithful in small tasks, God often increases our responsibilities and sphere of influence.

Nehemiah Wisely Counseled New Guards

Now that Hanani and Hananiah were in charge, Nehemiah gave them some specific instructions for supervising the newly assigned gatekeepers and city guards. He knew that gates and walls alone could not keep out the enemy. The city needed to adopt a wise defensive strategy as well.

Newly appointed gatekeepers were to open the city gates for just a few hours each day (7:3). Jerusalem, though rebuilt, was sparsely populated (7:4). Workers from other regions of Judah had gone home. Unwanted individuals could easily enter the city undetected if the gates weren't watched. Nehemiah planned for the city gates to be open only during the busy midday hours, when most of Jerusalem's populace would be out and about.

Newly appointed city guards were to keep watch around their neighborhoods night and day. This was a wise plan in that people are motivated to protect their own neighborhoods.

10. Read Nehemiah 7:3. Was Nehemiah showing a lack of faith in God with the cautious instructions he gave to the gatekeepers and guards?

11. Read Proverbs 22:3. What principle in this verse helps explain why Nehemiah thought it was necessary to appoint gatekeepers and guards?

Nehemiah Wisely Strategized a New Population

Jerusalem's population was sparse following the rebuilding project (7:4) because the city was still being developed. So, Nehemiah followed God's lead to implement a plan to populate the city. Nehemiah focused on attracting those of pure Jewish ancestry who could prove they would be loyal citizens. Nehemiah was obviously concerned about keeping out potential Samaritan spies.

The land area of the city itself was quite large. In fact, some scholars estimate that Jerusalem covered about 260 acres. Of the roughly 52,000 Jews who had returned to Judah under Zerubbabel and Ezra, few decided to settle in Jerusalem, probably because they felt defenseless without city walls. Thus, for several generations the Jews avoided building homes in Jerusalem.

Ezra's genealogical record assisted Nehemiah in ensuring Jerusalem had a purely Jewish population. Nehemiah's actions helped preserve the people's lineage as they anticipated the coming of the Messiah from the tribe of Judah. In addition, Nehemiah's actions prohibited entrance and residence to anyone who wanted to harm God's people and disrupt the city.

Ninety years before Nehemiah's return, Zerubbabel had taken a census of the initial returnees (Ezra 2). By using this list as a working document for his repopulation plan, Nehemiah provided some much-needed continuity for Jerusalem's past, present, and future. This directory listed some by clans, some according to their original communities, and others by profession or vocation. Those listed according to clan included the descendants of Parosh and seventeen other families (7:8–25). Those listed according to community included the men of Bethlehem and twelve other communities (7:26–38).

The following lists were given in the registry according to occupation: the priests (7:39–42), the Levites (7:43), the singers (7:44), the gatekeepers (7:45), the temple servants (7:46–56), the descendants of Solomon's servants (7:57–61), the descendants of Delaiah, Tobiah, and Nekoda (7:61, 62), and the undocumented priests (7:63–65).

The undocumented priests were unable to prove their ancestry. This posed a significant problem because the law of Moses insisted that a priest must be of the Levitical Aaronic line. It would have been presumptuous to expect God to bless leaders who failed to meet His requirements. Something had to be done.

12. What would be the wise, though not necessarily nice, decision to make regarding the undocumented priests?

13. Why can't a leader let his decisions be dictated by what would be the nice thing to do?

If all the undocumented priests had been automatically barred from their temple service, possibly some qualified priests would have lost their rightful ministry. For that reason, they were suspended "as polluted, put from the priesthood" (7:64; cf. Ezra 2:62). This suspension was temporary until the Urim and Thummim could be consulted (7:65; cf. Ezra 2:63). Through the Urim and Thummim, God would reveal which priests were clean and which priests were not.

Why did Nehemiah include all these details in his use of the registry? Perhaps he wanted to be reminded of the need for purity among God's leaders. Further, he certainly wanted to remind the people of his day that spiritual leaders must meet God's specified qualifications.

14. Creativity and vision are important qualities to look for in potential leaders. But why should those types of qualities not be the only criteria for appointing spiritual leaders?

After listing the returnees according to their various groupings, Nehemiah copied details from Ezra's census. He included the number of people and the fact that some gave to support the rebuilding process (7:66–72; Ezra 2:64–69).

Nehemiah 7 ends with all the people organized under Nehemiah's godly leadership (7:73). He stayed with the job until the end, completing all the details and taking care of the people involved.

Nehemiah 8 goes on to explore the exciting story of the renewal that took place within the rebuilt city. The inspired author, however, didn't rush ahead to that wonderful account without first completing the record of all that it took to consider the wall project complete and the city safe.

Nehemiah followed good problem-solving steps and thus made wise decisions. First, he determined the problem was the ongoing vulnerability of Jerusalem. Second, he exercised foresight, seeing Jerusalem being overrun by enemies if not protected. Third, he drew on others' wisdom by appointing Hanani and Hananiah as leaders. Fourth, he delegated resources by recommending helpers for Hanani and Hananiah and by checking Jerusalem's documents. Fifth, he drafted a solution by devising a plan for a defense system and for the repopulation procedure. Sixth, he carried out his plans by making appointments, giving instructions, and laying groundwork.

MAKING IT PERSONAL

15. How might you apply Nehemiah's problem-solving steps listed below?
    - Identify the problem.
    - Develop foresight.
    - Seek wisdom.
    - Delegate resources.
    - Draft a solution.
    - Do it!

16. Ask for God's help and direction concerning a specific problem you are facing that needs solving.

God's Word Is Powerful

Scripture Focus

Nehemiah 8

Theme

A spiritual leader shares God's Word with confidence.

Memory Verse

"For the word of God is quick, and powerful, and sharper than any twoedged sword, piercing even to the dividing asunder of soul and spirit, and of the joints and marrow, and is a discerner of the thoughts and intents of the heart" (Hebrews 4:12).

GETTING STARTED

Martin-Seymour Smith wrote a book called *The 100 Most Influential Books Ever Written*. In that book he listed what he thought were the top 100 influential books. Not surprisingly, the Old Testament and the New Testament both made his list. Some of the other books on his list were religious in nature. Those books included the Hindu scriptures called *Upanishads*, the Muslim *Quran*, and the Judaic mysticism religious writings called *Kabbalah*.

If this list were narrowed down to the books that are "alive," only the Old and New Testaments would make the list!

1. What do we mean when we say that the Bible is "alive"?

2. Describe a time when the Bible came "alive" to you.

3. How did you respond?

Though the Bible is alive, that does not mean that all we need to do is read it. We should be committed to studying it and meditating on it so we truly understand it and so God can use it to change our lives.

Ezra took time to explain the Scriptures as he read them to the Jews. As a result, the people understood the Scriptures and responded to them.

SEARCHING THE SCRIPTURES

Although the Jews had rebuilt the walls of Jerusalem and had established the community inside its walls, something else needed building. The people needed to build their understanding of God as revealed in His Word. As a sensitive leader, Nehemiah worked to facilitate the people's awareness and submission to God's Word.

Nehemiah Upheld God's Word

It was now Tishri, the seventh month (September/October) and the most sacred month of the Jewish year. During Tishri, the Jews celebrated the Feast of Trumpets (Tishri 1; Num. 29:1–6), the Day of Atonement (Tishri 10; Num. 29:7–11), and the Feast of Tabernacles or Booths (Tishri 15–21; Num. 29:12–40).

The Feast of Trumpets followed the time of harvest and included a memorial blowing of trumpets and a formal assembly. The Day of Atonement included a time for the people to sorrowfully reflect on their shortcomings. The Feast of Tabernacles focused on remembering Israel's deliverance from Egypt and their subsequent wandering in the wilderness for forty years.

After settling into their cities and homes, the people regathered at the Water Gate on the first day of the seventh month, the Jewish celebration of the Feast of Trumpets (8:2). Tishri 1 is the beginning of Israel's civil new year.

Supporting the Desire to Hear God's Word

A large assembly ("all the people") had gathered at the Water Gate to ask Ezra to read for them from the book of the law of Moses (8:1). They recognized the book as a record of God's commands to them.

4. Read Nehemiah 8:1, 2 and Psalm 1:2, 3. How did the people of Israel reflect the theme of Psalm 1:2 and 3?

5. When was the last time you were hungry to know God's Word?

As Bible-believing Christians, the basis of our faith is the written Word of God. We can increase our faith only by God's Word (Rom. 10:17). Thus, pastors should use expository preaching when communicating God's Word to their people (2 Tim. 4:2). Ezra modeled this word by word and verse by verse method of preaching in Nehemiah 8.

The completion of the wall was obviously a work of God through His willing servants. God's enabling caught the people's attention. They desired to know Him better through learning His Word.

6. When God works in obvious ways in your life, how does that affect your desire to know Him and live by His ways?

The crowd gathered at the Water Gate rather than at the temple because only men would have been allowed in the temple (8:2). God's important message through His Word is for all people of all ages (Deut. 31:12, 13).

Nehemiah realized that the law of Moses was not merely the words of Moses. Moses wrote these as the words "which the Lord had commanded to Israel" (8:1).

7. Read 2 Timothy 3:16, 17. How might a Christian show that he believes the Bible is God's Word?

Because he highly regarded God's Word, Nehemiah supported the people's request to hear Ezra read it. In fact, it is quite possible that the tall wooden platform constructed at this location for Ezra's use had already been built under Nehemiah's direction (8:4).

Nehemiah clearly did not feel threatened by Ezra. If anything, he graciously deferred to him. Nehemiah felt at home in the role God had assigned to him and was pleased to respect the role God had assigned to Ezra.

As a "scribe" (8:1), Ezra had devoted his life to the systematic study and exposition of the Scriptures (Ezra 7:6, 10–12). As a descendant of Aaron's third son, Ezra legitimately held the office of "priest" (8:2; Ezra 7:1–5). As a priest, Ezra represented the people to God in acts of sacred worship in the temple. When Ezra returned to Jerusalem in 458 BC, his central purpose was to introduce spiritual revival and reform by faithfully and carefully proclaiming the Word of God. He had been commissioned by Artaxerxes I to teach the Scriptures to the repatriated Jews (Ezra 7:25, 26). Nehemiah wisely recognized Ezra's gifts and office and utilized his skills.

Ezra emphasized the people's understanding (8:2). That emphasis led to a true life-changing revival among God's people.

8. What happens to spiritual decisions that were based on a strong emotional appeal rather sound teaching from God's Word?

9. Think back to the important spiritual decisions you have made. What part did emotion and what part did God's Word play in making your decision a lasting decision?

Listening Attentively to God's Word

In willing response to the request of the people, Ezra boldly read the law (8:3, 5, 8). Nehemiah carefully listened with the rest of the congregation.

10. Why is a leader not exempt from needing to hear God's Word preached?

Ezra read aloud from the scroll "from the morning until midday." As he read, the men, women, and children listened attentively (8:3). Perhaps as many as 30,000 to 50,000 people gathered to hear Ezra. Given the importance of his message, he stood on a high platform so everyone could see and hear him well (8:4). Thirteen other religious leaders stood with Ezra on the platform.

When Ezra took the scroll to open it, the crowd immediately stood to its feet (8:5). Apparently, they stood for the duration of the reading to show their reverence for God's Word. Not having personal copies of God's Word to read on their own made hearing the Word a special experience.

11. How would you respond if your pastor asked you to stand while he preached for several hours?

Displaying a spirit of adoration and worship to God, Ezra proclaimed, "Bless the Lord!" All the people answered in unison, "Amen! Amen," lifted their hands, bowed their heads, and worshiped the Lord with their faces to the ground (8:6). The message immediately moved the people to repentance.

After establishing a spirit of worship and submission, Ezra read the words of the law clearly and understandably. Since Moses wrote in Hebrew and many of the people probably spoke Aramaic, Ezra might have translated the text to increase the people's understanding.

Assisted by others, Ezra "gave the sense," or the interpretation of the Word, as he read (8:7, 8). Proper interpretation is vital to Bible study and teaching. Ezra and his associates properly interpreted Scripture by first observing what the text said and then explaining what the text meant. This simple process for understanding God's Word remains the same for us today, except we have the Holy Spirit to help in our understanding of a text.

12. Read 1 Corinthians 2:12–14. When have you sensed the Holy Spirit was helping you understand a passage of Scripture?

Nehemiah's Positive Challenge

Even the correct interpretation of God's Word, although essential, is not ultimately enough. The Word must be received with the correct attitude and then put into action.

13. How faithful are you at completing the four basic steps in authentic Bible-learning as listed below?
    - Information—What does it say?
    - Insight—What does it mean?
    - Attitude—How should I respond?
    - Action—What should I do?

14. What will a person take away from the Scriptures if his practice is to read them only until something strikes him as interesting?

While Nehemiah was neither a scribe nor a priest, he recognized the influence his position had among the people. He wanted to use this influence for their spiritual wellbeing. Because it was the Feast of Trumpets, the civil new year, and Nehemiah was Jerusalem's civil leader, he addressed the assembly. Nehemiah challenged the people to stop their crying (8:9) and respond with joy to God's Word (8:10).

Ezra's proclamation of the law had a powerful impact. Perhaps the magnitude of the captivity's significance was just now becoming apparent to some of the Jewish people. The gravity of their national disobedience struck them.

While Nehemiah was no doubt pleased with their sensitivity to the Lord and His Word, he did not want the people to fall into morbid introspection. God's will for Israel on the Feast of Trumpets was to rejoice in Him. Nehemiah called the people to let the Scriptural significance of the day triumph over their immediate emotional reaction to God's Word.

Nehemiah emphasized the joy of the Lord and told the people to go, eat the feast of celebration, and share with those in need (8:10). Everyone, then, could celebrate the feast with joy. Their introspection was to turn to fellowship and sharing with others.

15. How much will a believer grow spiritually if his only takeaway from God's Word is a list of his shortcomings?

The Levites supported what Nehemiah told the assembly (8:11) and the people took the counsel to heart (8:12). They celebrated the Lord's goodness and provided food and drink to those in need. God's Word made a tremendous impression on Jerusalem. With the help of Ezra, the Levites, and Nehemiah, the people experienced the full cycle of spiritual learning (information, insight, attitude, and action). While it can be said that the city was revived by the rebuilding of the walls, it might also be said that the people were revived by the proclamation of the Word.

The People's Positive Response

The people's good response to God's Word lasted beyond the holiday celebration. They demonstrated an ongoing willingness to obey God. So, the next day the head of every household met with Ezra and the Levites to hear more of God's Word (8:13). As they listened, they learned about the Feast of Booths (Tabernacles) and the command to celebrate it (8:14).

God commanded Israel to celebrate the Feast of Booths annually between the 15th day and the 21st day of the seventh month (Lev. 23:33–44). The feast commemorated God's provision for the people when He brought them out of Egypt and cared for them in the wilderness. In addition, it looked ahead to the time when God will dwell with His people in the millennial Kingdom (cf. Zech. 14:16-21).

Being the second day of Tishri, the people had two weeks to prepare for the celebration. According to the laws of celebration, the people were to make "booths" or shelters to use for this celebration.

Responding to God's Word again, the people went into nearby woods and brought back branches for making booths (8:15). They built booths throughout the city on the housetops, in the temple court, and at the public square by the Water Gate (8:16).

This Feast of Booths made all the people of Judah glad (8:17), especially since they had not celebrated the feast as a unified nation since the days of Joshua. The celebration gave Jerusalem the new start it so desperately needed. Ezra continued to read from the law of God daily throughout the week-long celebration because of the Word's positive effects (8:18).

16. Why does reading God's Word and obeying it make believers glad?

The celebration concluded with a solemn assembly on the eighth day. The people added the extra day to the Feast of Tabernacles in accordance with the law (8:18). The law called for a reading of the entire law every seventh year the Jews celebrated the feast (Deut. 31:9–13). The Jews elected to fulfill that requirement since it had been many years since anyone celebrated the feast.

God's Word brought spiritual renewal to Jerusalem. Today, too, spiritual renewal results from rekindled devotion to Scripture. When God's people revere and obey the Bible, righteousness pervades their lives and impacts society.

MAKING IT PERSONAL

17. Should you be giving the Bible more attention in your own personal life? Explain.

18. What actions could you take to build the Bible into your life?

19. Perhaps, like these Jews, we should set aside some special time, even if a holiday or a vacation is not imminent, to reconnect with God through His Holy Word. When will you seek to set aside time to seek God in His Word?

Set the Example!

LESSON 11

Scripture Focus

Nehemiah 9:1–38

Theme

A spiritual leader sets the right example.

Memory Verse

"Brethren, be followers together of me, and mark them which walk so as ye have us for an ensample" (Philippians 3:17).

GETTING STARTED

Someone once said, "Remember, people will judge you by your actions, not your intentions. You may have a heart of gold, but so does a hard-boiled egg." And Edmund Burke, an 18th century philosopher, said, "Example is the school of mankind, and they will learn at no other."

There is no escaping the truth of those statements. Our examples speak louder than our instructions.

1. Name three people who are following your example, whether you realize it or not.

2. Do those who follow leaders learn more from what their leaders teach or how their leaders live? Explain.

The testimony of our lives is much louder than the lessons from our lips. Nehemiah knew that principle well. He was a leader who taught godliness with his life.

SEARCHING THE SCRIPTURES

Nehemiah won the strong admiration of the people despite the presence of Tobiah's followers in Jerusalem. Nehemiah's followers showed their admiration for Nehemiah by copying five of his behaviors. Those behaviors are the focus of this lesson.

The People Fasted as Nehemiah Had

A solemn meeting closed the Feast of Booths on Tishri 22. The events of chapter 9 opened on Tishri 24. Those who lingered in Jerusalem after the feast fasted voluntarily.

It might seem odd that the people fasted and put on sackcloth and ashes so soon after a period of joyous feasting. Especially since Nehemiah had asked the people to rejoice instead of weep (8:9, 10). The solemn assembly at the end of the Feast of Booths probably provided the impetus for the fasting (8:18). Just as the forty years in the wilderness climaxed with the awesome responsibility to conquer the land, the Feast of Booths climaxed with the awesome responsibility to be wise stewards of the land freshly repossessed and fortified.

The people in Jerusalem had more than likely acquired the practice of fasting from Nehemiah (cf. Neh. 1:4). Upon first hearing of the devastation in Jerusalem from Hanani, Nehemiah set aside his own physical needs and desires and devoted himself to prayer to address the problem in Jerusalem.

3. How might a leader show his commitment to the Lord today?

4. Is fasting still an appropriate way for a leader to show his commitment to God? Explain.

5. Read Matthew 6:16–18. What instructions did Jesus give concerning fasting?

The People Mourned as Nehemiah Had

The people wore sackcloth and humbly placed "earth upon them" when they fasted (9:1b). Once again, they followed the pattern Nehemiah had set (cf. Neh. 1:4).

But why would the people mourn? They had rebuilt Jerusalem's walls, and they had just experienced revival. Even Nehemiah had recently proclaimed, "The joy of the Lord is your strength" (8:10).

The context explains the people's reason for mourning and fasting. Judah had indeed been restored, but it was not yet free (9:37). The land was still a province of Persia. It still owed taxes and loyalty to the Persian king. The people gained Persia's favor, but the favor was by no means permanent. The people even admitted, "We are in great distress" because of Persia (9:37).

It is good to bring our griefs before the Lord. Psalmists who lamented before God were not rebuked for doing so.

6. Read 1 Peter 5:7. What does this verse ask believers to do?

7. How does a leader affect those he leads when he publicly casts his cares on the Lord?

The People Confessed as Nehemiah Had

When Nehemiah first heard the news of Judah's plight, he confessed his sins and Judah's sins before the Lord. He prayed, "I . . . confess the sins of the children of Israel, which we have sinned against thee; both I and my father's house have sinned. We have dealt very corruptly against thee, and have not kept the commandments, nor the statutes, nor the judgments, which thou commandest thy servant Moses" (1:6b, 7). Nehemiah confessed these sins because he knew the sins had led to Jerusalem's chastisement.

Like Nehemiah, the people fasting in Jerusalem surely perceived their bondage to Persia as chastisement for their sin. Moses had warned God's people about experiencing discipline for rebellion against God (Deut. 28—30). The people took those warnings to heart.

To further show their return to God, the people separated themselves from all the non-Jews in the city and listened intently to the reading of the law for three hours (9:2, 3). For the following three hours, they confessed their sins before the Lord.

8. Does a leader help his people by pretending to be perfect and never needing to confess his sins? Explain.

9. What cautions might a leader use when confessing his sins before others?

The People Worshiped as Nehemiah Had

Worship was customary for Nehemiah. He repeated the worshipful title, "God of heaven," numerous times in his book (1:4; 1:5; 2:4; 2:20). He also took a strong role in leading the people in worship during the Feast of Trumpets and the Feast of Booths (chapter 8). It is not surprising, then, that the congregation of Jerusalem turned to God in spontaneous worship (9:3).

10. Describe the worship of a leader who is mostly interested in drawing attention to himself instead of God?

11. Why is worship something we can't convincingly pretend to do?

The People Prayed as Nehemiah Had

The prayer that followed the people's worship resembles the pattern of a descriptive praise psalm. The people, led by Levites, praised the Lord for Who He is and for what He had done (9:5–38).

Reading through the book of Nehemiah, we learn to appreciate the frequency with which Nehemiah prayed (1:4–11; 2:4; 4:1–5, 9; 5:19; 6:9, 14). This man of prayer had influenced the people of Jerusalem to be people of prayer. They prayed for God's power, providence, and provision.

12. Read Nehemiah 9:5, 6. Why is recognizing God as the creator a good place to start a worshipful prayer to God?

God's power is best seen in His ability to create something out of nothing. That ability gives Him the authority over all the earth. The Levites stated that the host of Heaven recognizes God's creative power and worships Him (9:6).

God's creative power also means His ability to help those who come to Him with needs is unlimited. In the past, Israel foolishly abandoned their creator for lifeless gods. The people of Nehemiah's day realized the futility of worshiping anything or anyone but God.

As the Levites moved into the body of their prayer, they retraced Israel's history beginning with the call of Abraham and God's unconditional Covenant with him (9:7, 8). They then moved on to discuss the Exodus, including God's deliverance of Israel through the Red Sea, His defeat of the Egyptians, and the direction and protection that He supplied to His children as they journeyed (9:9–12).

13. Read Nehemiah 9:7–12. What attributes and characteristics of God are evident in these verses?

The Levites next rehearsed God's revelation of the Mosaic Law at Mount Sinai and God's care for His people in the wilderness (9:13–15). If Israel obeyed the law, God would bless them. If they disobeyed, God promised to discipline them. God's promises associated with the Mosaic Covenant made it a conditional Covenant.

14. Read Nehemiah 9:13–15. What attributes and characteristics of God are evident in these verses?

15. How would you expect God's people to respond to such an awesome God?

God's people failed to obey the Mosaic Covenant throughout most of their history. The Levites specifically noted Israel's creation and worship of a golden calf (9:16–21).

16. Read Nehemiah 9:16–21. How did God respond to Israel's disobedience?

God remained true to the Abrahamic Covenant by leading His people to the doorstep of the Promised Land and then fighting for them as they took the land. They delighted themselves in God's goodness as they ate the fruit of the land (9:22–25).

Soon a generation who didn't know God rebelled against Him, cast God's law behind their backs, and killed God's prophets (9:26). Thus began an oft-repeated cycle of sin, repentance, and deliverance until God finally chased His rebellious people from the Promised Land (9:27–30).

17. Read Nehemiah 9:26–30. Which attributes of God were apparent in His treatment of His rebellious people?

18. Read Nehemiah 9:31–35. What one word would you use to describe God based on this passage?

The Levites leading the people in prayer emphasized that God remained faithful to His promises to Israel while His people didn't. The Levites included the current generation as guilty before God. They lived in the Promised Land again but only with Persian permission and Persian supervision. They enjoyed the fruit of the land but in a limited way. Being under Persian control meant life in the land was hard (9:36, 37).

The people under Nehemiah's leadership learned from God's Word both the awfulness of sin and the awesomeness of God. If they were going to continue in the land and begin to enjoy it more, they knew they must remain true to God.

The People Remembered as Nehemiah Had

When Nehemiah prayed at the beginning of his book, he based his request on God's covenant (Neh. 1:5–11). In fact, he specifically prayed to the "God, that keepeth covenant" (1:5). It is striking to note that in the people's prayer, they, too, prayed to the "God, who keepest covenant" (9:32). Notice also the similarity of 9:32 to Nehemiah's statement in 4:14. Evidently his emphasis had made an impact on those who had learned from his example. Nehemiah's theological concept of God took root in the people's hearts.

God cut a covenant with Abraham in Genesis 15. He also promised to give Abraham a land, a special offspring, and a worldwide blessing (Gen. 12:1, 2). This covenant was unconditional, literal, and eternal (Gen. 13:14, 15). It was reaffirmed to Moses in the Land Covenant (Deut. 30), reaffirmed to David in the Davidic Covenant (2 Sam. 7), and reaffirmed to Jeremiah in the New Covenant (Jer. 32).

As chapter 9 of Nehemiah concludes, the people of Jerusalem made a covenant with God to do all that He commanded them. Their covenant was based upon His covenants with them (9:38). The next lesson will give the details of that covenant, and the final lesson will reveal that the people failed to keep their promises. They proved again that no one can keep

God's laws perfectly. Salvation, then, has to come from outside humanity.

The answer to Israel's unfaithfulness is found way back in the promises God made to Abraham. He said that all the families of the world would be blessed through him (Gen. 12:3). That promise directly relates to the coming of Jesus as the God-Man in the line of Abraham (Gal. 3:8). Jesus died on the cross and rose again to provide the only solution to sin for all the families of the earth. Abraham had faith in God to save him from his sins (Gal. 3:6). He understood he was powerless to save himself. We, on this side of the cross, fully understand God's provision of salvation through Christ and put our faith in Him, knowing we too are powerless to solve our sin problem on our own.

MAKING IT PERSONAL

We lead with our entire lives, not with just our words. We can give godly instructions, but if we don't back them up with our lives, our instructions won't have an impact.

We should also remember that just as our salvation came through faith in Christ, so also our spiritual growth comes as we put our faith in God to strengthen us to say no to sin and yes to Him.

19. Identify two people you want to influence toward godliness.

20. What will you do to enhance your godly influence on their lives?

Trust and Obey

LESSON 12

Scripture Focus

Nehemiah 10; 11

Theme

A spiritual leader stimulates others to trust and obey God.

Memory Verse

"Who is among you that feareth the Lord, that obeyeth the voice of his servant, that walketh in darkness, and hath no light? let him trust in the name of the Lord, and stay upon his God" (Isaiah 50:10).

GETTING STARTED

Take a minute and say the pledge to your country's flag. Now say it again, but this time think about the pledge you are making. Let the words resonate in your mind.

Stopping to think about the words should give the pledge a fresh meaning in your mind.

Too often as believers we "pledge" our lives to God with about the same seriousness we have as we pledge to our country. God deserves our full, serious attention as we live for Him.

1. How serious are you when you say the pledge to our country's flag?

2. What difference does reciting the pledge make in your life?

Our ultimate allegiance should be to God. We ought to trust Him and therefore pledge to obey Him. This lesson provides an example of a pledge to God and a challenge to consider to whom we have pledged our lives.

SEARCHING THE SCRIPTURES

After God brought revival to Jerusalem's population through the public reading of the Scriptures (Neh. 8), the people conducted a spontaneous six-hour public prayer meeting (9:3). Such a meeting had not occurred since the dedication of Solomon's Temple (2 Chron. 6:12–42). At the conclusion of Jerusalem's heartfelt prayer, the people made a new commitment before the Lord (Neh. 9:38). Nehemiah 10 gives the details of that public commitment.

A Pledge of Obedience

The definition of a covenant is a formal binding agreement, a compact, or a contract. Probably the most common covenant that comes to mind is the covenant of marriage, which is a binding legal transaction. It includes witnesses and signed documentation. The covenant made by the Jews under Nehemiah's leadership was essentially a renewal of their pledge to keep the Mosaic Covenant. The Mosaic Covenant begins with the Ten Commandments in Exodus 19 and runs through Deuteronomy 28. The Covenant is conditional, meaning the Jews would receive God's blessing outlined in the Covenant if they obeyed the accompanying commandments. If they broke the commandments, they would experience the curses outlined in the Covenant.

Makers of the Oath

In the first section of chapter 10, Nehemiah records the names of all who signed the Covenant renewal. As the leader, Nehemiah signed it first (10:1). By signing the Covenant, he identified with the people of Jerusalem and publicly pledged his dependence upon God and his obedience to Him.

Following Nehemiah's lead, the other civil leaders and religious leaders put their seals to the agreement. Twenty-four princes and priests (10:1–8), seventeen Levites (10:9–13), and forty-four heads of families (10:14–27) signed the agreement. Since it was impossible for everyone to sign the document, the rest of the people aligned with these leaders by making a verbal oath (10:28, 29).

This was a very serious obligation that the people entered. Ecclesiastes 5:1–7 makes this concept clear, “Better is it that thou shouldest not vow, than that thou shouldest vow and not pay” (Eccl. 5:5).

While this vow was not foolish, it was serious. The people bound themselves “and entered into a curse, and into an oath, to walk in God’s law, which was given by Moses the servant of God, and to observe and do all the commandments” (Neh. 10:29).

Such public commitments were related to the fact that the Old Testament people of God were a nation living together in covenant with Him. As mentioned already, the Jews were committing to obey the Mosaic Covenant that was already binding upon them.

As church age believers, we aren’t under the Mosaic Covenant in that the specific blessings and cursing attached to God’s commandments were only for the Jews. Many of God’s commands in the Mosaic Covenant, however, including all but one of the Ten Commandments, are repeated in the New Testament. God wants us to obey those commands out of love for Him. Our obedience brings us blessings like peace, joy, and contentment but not the bountiful rains or bumper crops promised in the Mosaic Covenant (Deut. 28:1–14). If we disobey God, He will chasten us in various ways to get our attention and draw us back to Him (Heb. 12:5–7), but we won’t necessarily experience drought or be kicked out of our homes (Deut. 28:15–68).

Though we aren’t under the Mosaic Covenant, we should always abide by the commitments we make through our words in the course of all kinds of conversation. Jesus emphasized this in Matthew 5:33–37, and James reiterated this concept in James 5:12.

3. Read James 5:12. Summarize the principle of this verse.

The apostle Peter attempted to make grandiose claims on occasion (cf. Matt. 26:35; Mark 14:31; Luke 22:33), but learned through experience that these statements were easier to make than to keep, and far less important than obedience without presumption (cf. Luke 22:34; 54–62).

Terms of the Oath

The bottom line of the pledge that the people in Nehemiah’s time made to God is recorded in the second half of Nehemiah 10:29.

Jerusalem's citizens promised to observe and do all the commandments of the Lord, including God's moral, civil, and ceremonial laws. In both Nehemiah's prayer (1:7) and the people's prayer (9:34), those praying confessed that they had violated all three aspects of God's law.

As the people came off their experiences in chapters 8 and 9, the types of sins that had brought the Babylonian Captivity on the nation were foremost on their minds. Thus, they made this pledge that dealt with marriage (10:30), the observation of the Sabbath Day and Sabbatical Year (10:31), the care of the house of God, and the matters of offerings and the giving of firstfruits and tithes (10:32–39).

In taking this solemn oath, the people pledged themselves to their own curse and thereby recognized God's chastisement for disobedience as outlined in the Mosaic Covenant.

God had specifically commanded the people of Israel not to intermarry with those who were not the covenant people (Exod. 34:14–16). He did so to preserve their spiritual purity. Nevertheless, intermarriage became a besetting sin for Israel. They fell into this sin not long after occupying the Promised Land. God faithfully judged them according to the Mosaic Covenant (Judg. 3:5–8). During the period of monarchy, Solomon led the nation into chaos and schism as a result of his blatant disobedience to God's laws governing marriage (1 Kings 10—12). Even when the people returned to Jerusalem from captivity, they brought this sin with them (Ezra 9; 10). We saw in the book of Nehemiah the disastrous results this behavior brought on God's people (6:17–19). The nation never seemed to learn from her past sins.

4. Why would it have been tempting for the Jews to intermarry with pagans as they returned from captivity?

5. Read 1 Corinthians 6:14—7:1. What did Paul say concerning intermarrying with unbelievers?

In the law, God commanded the people of Israel to keep the Sabbath day holy as a day of rest (Exod. 20:8–11). Motivated by greed and selfish ambition, the people had frequently violated this law. They valued material gain over their identification with the Lord of the Sabbath. They pledged to observe the Sabbath just as God required (Neh. 10:31).

The Jews understood that it had been due in part to their violation of the law of the seventh-year Sabbath (Lev. 25:1–7) that God allowed the Babylonians to take them captive. God had warned His people that there would be one year of captivity for every year of failure to institute this law (2 Chron. 36:20, 21).

6. God does not now require believers to keep the Sabbath, but how might greed and selfish ambition show themselves in a believer's life today?

In the final specific pledge of the agreement, the people promised to support God's work financially (Neh. 10:32–39). They promised to give the temple an annual offering of a third of a shekel (10:32). God's law required an annual offering of half a shekel (cf. Exod. 30:11–16), suggesting that the Jews didn't think they could afford God's minimum requirement.

Offerings received at the temple provided for the showbread, sacrifices, feasts, and other services (Neh. 10:33). The Lord's work depended on the faithful giving of God's people.

Other promises included the contribution of wood to burn on the altar of sacrifice (cf. Lev. 6:12, 13), the bringing of the firstfruits of crops and trees (cf. Exod. 23:19), and the dedication of their firstborn sons and animals (Exod. 22:29; Deut. 12:6).

7. What is the correlation between a person's faith in God and his giving?

The final words of the Jews' oath sum up all that the people had covenanted to do together: "We will not forsake the house of our God" (Neh. 10:39).

8. What does dedication to God mean for us as church-age believers who are not under the law but under grace?

An Act of Trust: Settlement in Jerusalem

When Nehemiah laid the groundwork for the city's resettlement (Neh. 7), he must have known the timing was not right. After the nation's renewal (Neh. 8—10), the people were ready for the repopulation phase of Nehemiah's plan.

Obedience and trust work together. Having renewed their commitment to the Lord, the people were ready to repopulate the city of Jerusalem. Their confession of sins and promises to observe the law put their minds at ease. They no longer feared an enemy attack as part of God's chastening hand.

The rulers who dwelt at Jerusalem (11:1) were there primarily to maintain the temple. By casting lots, the leaders determined who else should be included in the ten percent of Judah's population to relocate inside the rebuilt holy city (11:1).

The use of lots prevented favoritism or inequity in such a serious choice. All those who were selected no doubt accepted this as God's sovereign will, for they moved to Jerusalem willingly (11:2).

A total of 3,044 men and their families moved from the general region of Judah to inside the city walls of Jerusalem. These included 468 from the tribe of Judah, 928 from the tribe of Benjamin, 1,192 priests, 284 Levites, and 172 porters or gatekeepers. Nehemiah's careful plan had finally been implemented.

An Act of Trust: Settlement near Jerusalem

Others of the tribe of Judah settled in seventeen towns and communities near Jerusalem (11:25–30). Some settled as far south as Beersheba, thirty-two miles away.

North of Judah, some of the tribe of Benjamin settled in fifteen towns and villages (11:31–35). The remaining Levites settled in both regions (11:36). Nehemiah certainly exercised grace along with his regulatory plan.

Everything appeared to be in perfect order within the rebuilt city except for the fact that each person was still a sinner. No doubt they began to compromise and break God's commands soon after their pledge to obey them.

9. When have you failed to keep a promise you made to God?

10. To what did you attribute your failure?

11. Why can't we count on our good intentions as the impetus for spiritual growth in our lives?

12. What can we count on for change in our lives?

MAKING IT PERSONAL

13. In what ways do you need to grow spiritually in your life?

14. What steps will you take to facilitate growth in those areas of your life?

Spiritual growth will not take place outside of God's grace. A promise to grow will not automatically translate into actual growth. As we put our faith in Him and seek Him through His Word and prayer, He empowers us through His Spirit to grow.

15. Commit to seek God's help to overcome any besetting sins (Heb 12:1).

Compromising Again

LESSON 13

Scripture Focus

Nehemiah 12; 13

Theme

A spiritual leader guides others into dedication and separation to God.

Memory Verses

"Blessed is the man that walketh not in the counsel of the ungodly, nor standeth in the way of sinners, nor sitteth in the seat of the scornful. But his delight is in the law of the LORD; and in his law doth he meditate day and night" (Psalm 1:1, 2).

GETTING STARTED

In an hour or two of watching television, you may see an ad or two for a weight loss program, especially in January. Those ads, however, are always followed by commercials for candy bars, fast food, or ice cream. We only have to look at our waistlines to determine which ads are more appealing and effective!

1. If you were on a diet, what food would tempt you the most to compromise your diet?

2. What special steps might you take to keep from eating that food?

Nehemiah celebrated the dedication of the wall of Jerusalem with the Jews before he went back to visit the king of Persia. When he returned from Persia, he found that many of the Jews had compromised. He dealt with their sin as a wise leader.

SEARCHING THE SCRIPTURES

For the people of Jerusalem to build 2.6 miles of tall city walls in a period of 52 days was a monumental accomplishment in the strength and grace of God (Neh. 6:16). This called for a spectacular celebration! Having just gone through a purging process of spiritual revival, the people wanted this to be a God-honoring celebration as well. Unfortunately, this is not the end of the story. After Nehemiah went back to Persia and later returned to Judah, he discovered that the people were back to their old sins. He therefore concluded his ministry with an urgent appeal for separation from evil.

Dedication of the Walls

As a good leader, Nehemiah honored faithful servants of the Lord. He gave the names of those serving in the temple in chapter 12. First, he listed the post-exilic temple leaders. His recognition of these men reveals his understanding of Jerusalem. The wall of Jerusalem received its importance because of what it protected—God's holy temple! He included the leaders of the priests (12:1–7), the priests' helpers (12:8, 9), the high priests (12:10, 11), the heads of the priestly families (12:12–21), and other Levites and priestly associates (12:22–26).

Nehemiah 12:27–47 continued the historical narrative from 11:2. Although the walls had been finished for some time (6:15), dedication ceremonies were not held until Jerusalem was successfully reestablished. At this stage Nehemiah could also celebrate the completion of his task. As the dedication ceremonies were planned, emphasis was placed on the service as a rendering of thanks to God (12:31).

The purpose of the celebration is given in 12:27. Levites were enlisted to provide music of "gladness" (12:27–29). Both vocalists and instrumentalists were summoned to provide songs of thanksgiving and praise, using cymbals, psalteries, and harps" (12:27).

Before the actual dedication could begin, both the walls and the worshipers had to be ceremonially cleansed (12:30). Priests, Levites, and the general Jewish public were all cleansed. Nehemiah seems to indicate that the blood of animal sacrifices was sprinkled on the walls and gates.

3. Read Nehemiah 12:30. Why was it important to dedicate the people before dedicating the wall?

4. What implications does this have for today as we seek to do the Lord's work?

Nehemiah took a major role in planning this spectacular dedication. He appointed two choirs of thanksgiving to encircle the city on top of the walls. Both choirs were evidently to start at the Valley Gate, the same gate through which Nehemiah first passed to view the city on his nighttime inspection (2:13).

Ezra led one of these choirs. This choir included Hoshaiah, half of the leaders, and priests with trumpets and other instrumentalists. At the signal, this group marched counterclockwise around the city on top of the wall (12:31–37).

The other group included Nehemiah, half of the officials, priests with trumpets, and other singers. This group marched clockwise around the city on the wall at the same time (12:38–42).

What an experience of worship and celebration this must have created. It not only directed Jerusalem's praise to God for the new wall, but it also gave a powerful testimony to all the onlookers surrounding the city. Perhaps even Tobiah was watching.

5. Read Nehemiah 4:3. What did Tobiah say about the wall as the Jews were building it?

6. How do you think he reacted when he saw large groups of Jews walking on the wall?

The two choirs evidently met inside the city walls and completed their elaborate dedication ceremony at the temple with the offering of many sacrifices. "That day they offered great sacrifices, and rejoiced: for God had made them rejoice with great joy: the wives also and the children rejoiced" (12:43). Such "great joy" resounded that the noise of celebration was heard at great distances (12:42, 43).

7. What connection do you see between the completed walls and the great joy the people had?

8. When have you seen the connection between obedience to God and great joy in your life?

9. What happens to our level of joy when we try to avoid serving God, particularly service that requires serious dedication?

At the conclusion of the service, Nehemiah directed the people in the giving of contributions, firstfruits, and tithes, just as they had promised to do in the oath recorded in chapter 10. Temple workers received what they needed, and all the holy vessels were "sanctified." With the completion of the wall and the reconstructing of Jerusalem, the temple of God also got a fresh start.

Separation from Pagans

Nehemiah's first term as governor had been most successful. During the twelve years of that term (445–433 BC; Neh. 5:14), he had rebuilt a strong civil and moral foundation for Judah's future. His long tenure demonstrated a genuine commitment to Jerusalem's welfare and not just a passing interest. However, he finally returned to Persia, probably to fulfill the promise he had made to Artaxerxes I (cf. 2:6; 13:6).

In Nehemiah's absence, the people of Jerusalem quickly lapsed into their old sinful ways. The prophet Malachi confronted them for their backsliding (Mal. 1:6—3:12).

10. Read Malachi 1:6–14; 2:17; 3:1–5. How does Malachi characterize the Jews' service for God?

11. What was the Jews' basic problem (see 3:5)?

12. Have you had times in your life when you just went through the motions of serving God without reverencing Him? Explain.

Nehemiah was shocked when he returned to Judah for his second term as the governor-in-chief (Neh. 13:7, 8).

Nehemiah discovered a flagrant violation of the laws of Moses. Jews were inviting Ammonites and Moabites to worship at the holy temple! Historically, these tribes had tried to bar the children of Israel from possessing the Promised Land (Deut. 23:3–6). They even tried to curse Israel with the help of the false prophet Balaam (Num. 22—25). Nehemiah boldly had these portions of the law read to the people once again, and immediately they corrected the matter (Neh. 13:1–3).

Separation from Compromise

Nehemiah further discovered that Eliashib, the high priest, had invited Tobiah, the enemy of Jerusalem, to live in the temple. There, in one of the storerooms that once housed "meat offerings, the frankincense, and the vessels, and the tithes of the corn, the new wine, and the oil," Eliashib helped Tobiah set up housekeeping (13:4, 5).

Nehemiah became furious when he saw what had happened. He knew from personal experience that Tobiah was not only an Ammonite, but he was also an enemy of Jerusalem and of the true God (2:10, 19; 4:3; 6:1–14). Now Tobiah could oppose the work of God from within the temple.

13. What message would Eliashib have sent to the Jews when he made such arrangements for Tobiah?

Nehemiah must have been deeply puzzled at Eliashib's compromise, for he knew that Eliashib had helped to rebuild the wall during Tobiah's opposition. It was Eliashib the high priest who had rebuilt the Sheep Gate (see 3:1). Perhaps 13:4 gives the explanation. Tobiah and Eliashib may have been related to each other. If so, here is more evidence that pagan intermarriage produces tragic consequences.

According to Nehemiah 13:8 and 9, Nehemiah took immediate action. He stormed the storeroom and threw out all of Tobiah's "household stuff." This was followed by immediate ceremonial cleansing and the return of the room to temple service.

Separation from Worldly Materialism

One reason Tobiah could live in a temple storeroom was that many of these storerooms were empty (13:5). People had stopped giving to the work of God. Temple supplies had run low, and many Levites and temple servants had to work elsewhere to avoid starving to death (13:10). Thus, the ongoing sin of financial neglect was compounded by the neglecting of the temple servants. Furthermore, with the Levites absent from their temple service, the temple programs most likely suffered.

How quickly the people of Jerusalem forgot their oath, "We will not forsake the house of our God" (Neh. 10:39b). They distinctly violated every area of the promises they had made in Nehemiah 10:29–39.

Again, Malachi rebuked the people sharply for their lack of giving during this period of time (cf. Mal. 3:8–12).

14. Read Malachi 3:8–12. What point did God make about Himself?

15. What should we think about the notion that a believer could gain something of greater value by being disobedient to God?

Nehemiah confronted this problem too. The situation called for rededication and for accountability to God's law through His appointed leaders. He immediately appointed four temple leaders to oversee the giving of tithes and offerings (Neh. 13:13). And again, he prayed (13:14).

Interestingly, Nehemiah had to confront another issue that was linked with financial greed. The people had gone back on their word as they began to "profane the sabbath day" (13:17). Apparently, Jerusalem's population was more concerned about making money than keeping the Sabbath. As Nehemiah walked around the town one Sabbath, he saw Jews buying and selling and transporting the merchandise of craftsmen (13:15–18). All the markets were open and busy just as they were on any other day of the week.

Nehemiah probably remembered the oath the people had taken to keep the Sabbath (10:31). He immediately provided a remedy as governor, and his reaction was swift.

16. Read Nehemiah 13:17–22. How would you describe the actions Nehemiah took in dealing with the Sabbath violators? Was he being a wise leader?

First, Nehemiah confronted the people for profaning the Sabbath (13:17). He reminded them that this activity was the very cause for which God brought the captivity on Judah (13:18). Jeremiah had even prophesied that such chastisements—brought by fire like they were by the Babylonians and the Samaritans (Neh. 1:3; Jer. 39:8)—could be expected in return for this type of behavior (Jer. 17:19–27).

Second, he ordered that all the city gates be kept shut on the Sabbath (Neh. 13:19). Third, he appointed guards to see to it that no hucksters came near the city. Finally, Nehemiah threatened to personally throw any huckster away from the city walls who failed to comply with these regulations (13:20, 21).

Separation from Godless Intermarriage

The last paragraph of Nehemiah's book reveals that this brokenhearted spiritual leader had to deal again with Israel's besetting sin of intermarriage with pagans. Despite the commitment they solemnly sealed with God, promising never to fall into this sin again (10:30), the people gave their children in marriage to Ashdodites, Ammonites, and Moabites (13:23, 24).

17. Read Nehemiah 13:25–28. What did Nehemiah do to deal with the Jews' intermarriage with pagans?

18. What do his actions say about the seriousness of the sin?

Remembering their oath, and that they swore to their own curse, Nehemiah held them to it by calling down these curses on them (13:25). His confrontation was strong and powerful (13:26, 27). When he discovered that the high priest's grandson had married Sanballat's daughter, he "chased him" out of his sight (13:28). Nehemiah refused to tolerate sin and spiritual erosion.

This section gives tremendous teaching on the importance of maintaining a godly marriage, home, and family. It must be viewed in context, however, and in seeking to apply it we must consider it carefully in light of further revelation given in the New Testament for this present age.

In the New Testament age, God's people are likewise forbidden from marrying unbelievers, although unlike Old Testament times, there is no ethnic component involved in the guidelines for an acceptable marriage (cf. 1 Cor. 7:39). Also, the New Testament specifically counsels that a believer who is currently married to an unbeliever is not to seek a divorce simply because his or her spouse is not a Christian (1 Cor. 7:12–14).

After cleansing the priesthood and reappointing the temple leaders to their rightful tasks, Nehemiah closed his book in a manner so characteristic of this great man—he prayed (13:31). He can rightly be called a spiritual man and a leader.

MAKING IT PERSONAL

19. Why do believers compromise and grasp for what they shouldn't have as believers?

20. Have you compromised and followed particular sins? If so, deal with them with the same seriousness Nehemiah had in dealing with them.

As you conclude this amazing book of Nehemiah, you should have a newfound understanding and appreciation of the post-exilic history of the nation of Judah. By including this extensive report in His inspired Word, God showed the importance of these times and the many lessons He wants you to learn.

The book began with Nehemiah's brokenness as God's chosen leader to rebuild Jerusalem. His brokenness paved the way for the building of the walls and the restoration of the Jews.

Your spiritual growth begins with brokenness too. If you are living away from God, He wants you to respond first by confessing your sins. He then will start the reconstruction process in your life and will be able to make you into the type of believer and leader He wants you to be.